10 YEARS OF THE
OSPREYS

10 YEARS OF THE OSPREYS

Peter Owen

First impression: 2013

© Copyright Peter Owen and Y Lolfa Cyf., 2013

The contents of this book are subject to copyright, and may
not be reproduced by any means, mechanical or electronic,
without the prior, written consent of the publishers.

The publishers wish to acknowledge the support of
Cyngor Llyfrau Cymru

Cover design: Y Lolfa

All photographs included in this book are the copyright of
Ospreys Rugby and/or the various official photographers
employed by Ospreys Rugby over the last ten years:

Dave Dow/Dragon Tales Rugby;
Adam Davies/UK Press Photo; Huw Evans Agency.

ISBN: 978 184771 740 5

Published and printed in Wales
on paper from well maintained forests by
Y Lolfa Cyf., Talybont, Ceredigion SY24 5HE
website www.ylolfa.com
e-mail ylolfa@ylolfa.com
tel 01970 832 304
fax 832 782

Introduction

As **we celebrate ten** years of regional rugby, and with it ten years of the Ospreys, it's only right that we take the opportunity to look back and reflect on how far we have come as an organisation in such a short period of time.

When asked to contribute an introduction to this book I thought long and hard about where we started off back in 2003, what we have achieved on and off the field along the way, where we stand today, and what the future may hold for Ospreys Rugby.

You have to remember that ten years ago Welsh rugby was not in a healthy state. Everybody could see that change was needed but the reality was that all the negotiations, with the other clubs and with the Welsh Rugby Union, were really going nowhere. Nobody wanted to give up what they had – even if what they had had no foreseeable future.

David Moffett, WRU Chief Executive at the time, was very forthright with his views on the matter and he's since been proven right. What really brought the situation home to me was when he asked, "Well, you have nine professional clubs in Wales. How many are there in South Africa? Australia? New Zealand?" In 2003, there were just twelve senior professional outfits representing those three nations. New Zealand had

five; there were four in South Africa and just three in Australia.

"And you want nine?" he asked.

Those countries were light years ahead of us, rugby-wise, and his comments really hit home.

As discussions continued there were various suggestions and solutions put forward. Even after it was agreed to reduce the number, there were so many possible combinations of merging clubs and stand-alones, but he always preached that the end result should be a reduced number of teams representing geographic regions.

To cut a very long story short, eventually there was a mutual feeling between Neath and Swansea that the idea of setting up a new entity together could work. We thought it was a natural fit, bringing together two clubs in a region that broadly represented the old West Glamorgan.

Straight away everyone said that this region would be the one to fail. We were absolutely determined to prove the doubters wrong.

Prior to this, the dealings between the two clubs were minimal really, other than on the field. Mike Cuddy at Neath and myself at Swansea were charged with making this thing work, and, from day one we set about grasping the regional concept. We set ourselves up to be a proper, representative region as opposed to simply an amalgamation of two clubs and, looking back now, I think that was the key to our success. It set us on the right road.

We wanted a new identity from the very beginning. However, the guidelines laid down by the Union stressed that the regions had to be owned by the clubs involved, and we had to identify the fact it was Neath and Swansea.

Our stance from the very beginning was that we needed our own regional identity that wasn't linked to the clubs, hence naming the region the Ospreys. It made people sit up and take notice straight away; it was something absolutely unique. There were connotations to the coastal nature of the area with it being a sea eagle, which had also featured on the Swansea centenary crest. There was a genuine belief that it was something that people could buy into.

Obviously, we were the Neath Swansea Ospreys to begin with but before too long, as we became more established, we were simply the Ospreys. Our aim was to be identified as a region and we got there more quickly than we could have hoped. The phrase 'one true region' came to be associated with us and it's a phrase I think still holds true today.

Deciding team colours proved to be a very contentious and emotional issue for many people. To us it was a practical decision; black is the best fashion colour so we decided on that, with white as the change shirt. The choices reflected Neath and Swansea, but it wasn't as key to us as it maybe was to others.

From a business point of view the first two years,

when we played out of two grounds, were very difficult and it took a lot of effort from a lot of people to keep the ship afloat. It was a struggle, undoubtedly, but we had a sea change in our fortunes, come 2005.

Winning the league in only our second season of existence was an incredible achievement, something that everybody involved in those difficult early days should be enormously proud of. Prior to the first season we'd had just three months to put a squad together, so to win the league from a standing start so quickly was amazing.

Moving to the new stadium in 2005 on the back of winning the league really catapulted us forward at an incredible speed. It gave us facilities that are up there with the best in the rugby world and offered a far more welcoming environment for rugby supporters in the region who perhaps had no strong affiliation to the old clubs, Neath and Swansea, and who wanted something more modern than tired, run-down venues with history but not much else.

People began to identify that the Ospreys were a force to be reckoned with. Not just an organisation that had ambition, but ambition that was based on a regional philosophy.

There's no doubt that 2005 was the turning point for us and we built from there.

In the eight years since that first title we have led the way in Wales. There have been a further three league titles and an EDF Energy Cup win at Twickenham. We have produced and supplied more players than anyone else to the Welsh team during a particularly golden period for the national side with three Grand Slams in seven years and a Rugby World

Cup semi-final. Indeed, that second Grand Slam in 2008 was built on a win against England where an incredible 13 of the starting 15 were Ospreys players.

Most recently, five of our players went on the successful 2013 British & Irish Lions tour to Australia with Alun Wyn Jones, a born and bred Ospreylian and product of our development pathway, captaining the team in the series winning third Test.

We are immensely proud of all the achievements listed, but I speak for all our directors when I say that what gives us most pleasure is seeing one of our players coming through the ranks to wear the Ospreys shirt, and in many cases to then represent the nation. Underpinning our regional philosophy at all times has been an ethos of development and we've remained true to that constantly, right up to the present day.

Of course, the move to the Liberty Stadium allowed us to not only develop players, many of whom became world class, it also meant we were able to attract world-class players here to supplement our developmental programme, who we were proud to see in an Ospreys shirt.

While this was, again, something that helped establish us as a recognisable, leading brand in the global game, the world of professional sport is an ever-changing and evolving one and we have had to realign ourselves in recent years. This has proven to be the start of another chapter in our history.

All the time though, we have undoubtedly remained true to our belief in developing local players and coaches.

How would I rate the first ten years?

I would say that we have definitely over achieved, establishing ourselves as a recognised brand in world rugby, we have achieved on the field in respect of both trophies won and players provided to the Welsh team, and we have most definitely achieved in our fundamental belief in developing our own players and, latterly, developing coaches. That is something which is absolutely integral to our future, as better coaches make better players, it's as simple as that, and is the key to us continuing to develop players for many seasons to come.

We have arguably achieved just as much off the field.

In our formative years the business was very much driven by Mike Cuddy and myself, with invaluable and much needed support from the likes Geoff Atherton, Rob Davies and Mike James, rugby people to the core who share the regional vision. Latterly, Andrew Hore has brought rugby intelligence and an alternative outlook to the organisation, enabling us to turn that vision into reality.

What is important to stress is that we are no longer just Neath and Swansea. When the WRU agreed that regions didn't have to be owned by the clubs any longer, it allowed us to take the opportunity to introduce fresh minds, and fresh finance, to the organisation, restructuring ourselves into the entity we are today, which is Ospreys Rugby Ltd.

We are now at the stage where we have matured off the field, have a new executive and managerial structure, and while the original board members remain part of what we are doing, our outlook is now far wider than ever before.

Rugby as a professional sport is still very much in

its infancy, but it is a rapidly evolving business. New challenges crop up constantly; today the key challenge is the salaries available elsewhere, in France and England.

Economically, Wales is a very different place to either of those and we'll never compete financially – we need to act smarter, which is where our development philosophy with a well-established pathway can make a huge difference to our ongoing sustainability as we attempt to deal with the current challenges we face.

It's incredibly difficult to predict the future, as professional rugby is an ever-moving feast. What we've got to do is surround the organisation with talented, hard-working people who have the ability to adapt to whatever the ground rules are. We adapted to change in 2003 but, thankfully, we didn't stand still. We continued evolving and will continue to do so.

It's important to remember though, that without the past there is no future. As I wrote at the very beginning, our tenth anniversary gives us the perfect opportunity to reflect with pride on what we have achieved together so far. This book is the perfect way to do just that, providing a historic and statistical analysis of what has been an incredible journey.

I'm sure that every Ospreys supporter will enjoy being reminded of the ups and downs of the first ten years, and once they've devoured all the information contained within these pages will be eager to see what lies in store for us over the next ten years.

Roger Blyth
Chairman, Ospreys Rugby Ltd.

1

The summer of 2003 was to be one of great change in Welsh sport, with the onset of regional rugby.

The game had gone professional shortly before the turn of the century, and Wales was being left behind. A small playing base was being spread too thinly between the nine top-flight clubs, and with both the clubs and the national team struggling to make an impact something radical was needed – and regional rugby certainly was radical.

National Coach, Graham Henry, had been one of the first to raise concern when he proposed the creation of four elite teams, West Wales, South-East Wales, the South Wales Valleys and Gwent in December 2001, based on the franchise system in his native New Zealand.

Although nothing was to come of his suggestions, his successor as Wales Head Coach, Steve Hansen, also spoke up in support of such a system following his appointment in February 2002.

It was clear to everyone that change was needed, but nobody knew what that change should be. Towards the end of the 2001/02 season, the suggestion from the 'gang of six' – Bridgend, Cardiff, Llanelli, Newport, Pontypridd and Swansea – was for a reduction of the number of clubs playing in the top flight of Welsh rugby, the Premiership, from nine to six.

Their proposal found favour in the higher echelons of the WRU, recognising the need for drastic action, and it was put to the vote at an extraordinary general meeting of member clubs.

As the saying goes, turkeys wouldn't vote for Christmas, and sensing their pathway to the top division was being blocked, the motion was overwhelmingly kicked out by the clubs who voted 325 to 98 against.

The late Sir Tasker Watkins, then President of the WRU, admitted that the vote had left Welsh rugby at an all-time low: "Unless changes are made we'll never recover from this," he commented following the meeting.

Discussions continued well into 2002 and still there was no solution, as the domestic game faced collapse amidst indifference from the paying public, who were walking away in droves as attendances at Premiership matches fell to the hundreds in some cases.

December 2002 saw David Moffett, WRU Chief Executive, and Terry Cobner, Director of Rugby at the Union, host a meeting with the nine Premiership clubs to outline plans for a new provincial system. Proposed changes would see four sides, owned by the WRU, competing at the top level with the clubs acting as

What does it mean? The now familiar Ospreys 'mask' logo sprung up across Neath and Swansea ahead of the region's opening game — and nobody knew what it meant

feeder teams and providing their best players to the provinces.

The proposals, which would have seen a West Wales team based at Llanelli's Stradey Park, Mid Wales playing from Cardiff Arms Park, East Wales at Rodney Parade in Newport, and a North Wales side, whose home would be Wrexham FC's Racecourse Ground, were rejected out of hand.

In response, the clubs drew up an alternative proposal where clubs would come together as a partnership for European rugby. Still there were issues though, as Llanelli were keen to stand-alone, rather than combine forces with Swansea, while Neath also rejected the opportunity to form a partnership with the All Whites having already agreed in principle to join up with Bridgend.

The political machinations continued behind the scenes, and by the end of January 2003 six of the nine Premiership clubs had agreed a plan for four regional franchises that would compete in an expanded, season-long Celtic League and in Europe. Below that level would be an increased, 16-team Premiership.

Caerphilly, the minnows of the Premiership, were not included in the new framework, while Cardiff and Llanelli were opposed to the plan, claiming that it was not in the best interests of Welsh rugby.

Four weeks later, at another extraordinary general meeting of the WRU, the changes were this time voted in, despite the ongoing threat of legal action from Llanelli.

At the end of March, the Stradey club did indeed issue proceedings against the Union, claiming that they were both acting unlawfully in breaching a contractual ten-year agreement with the clubs that was signed just six years earlier and, also, were in breach of European competition law.

Just three days later though, in an unexpected twist, the WRU announced that agreement had been reached with the clubs and that for the 2003/04 season, a new five-team regional structure would be implemented.

Cardiff and Llanelli would stand alone while three new teams would be established by way of mergers, with the clubs involved owning 50 per cent each. Neath and Swansea would combine, Bridgend and Pontypridd, and finally, Ebbw Vale and Newport. It was progress, but it seemed to many observers to be more like a compromise, a halfway house with clubs and regions playing alongside each other in the same structure rather than the radical change that had been demanded.

Nevertheless, with just months to go until the new entities would kick-off their inaugural season, there was no time to waste.

Two former giants of the Welsh domestic game, Neath RFC and Swansea RFC, were now as one. Sworn rivals of old, the merger would never work. Or so they said.

Public meetings were held, in both Neath and Swansea, to gauge public reaction to the new entity and to outline plans for the future. A turbulent evening at the aptly named Revolution Bar gave a clear indication of the discontent among the traditional support base. Names were suggested and discarded. Eventually, after an evening of discussion at Swansea's St Helen's home, it was decided upon Neath Swansea Ospreys.

The osprey is a bird with a long association with both

rugby and the local community, albeit unrecognised by the wider public, featuring on both the Swansea RFC centenary crest and, since 1922, on the coat of arms of the town and then city of Swansea.

Sometimes known as a sea hawk or eagle, the osprey is bird of prey, a formidable predator that succeeds by a combination of style, skill and aggression, making it a perfect symbol for the new team, its white colouring and black eye-stripe reflecting the make-up of the two founding teams' traditional colours.

As the new season approached, Neath's Lyn Jones was appointed as Head Coach of the fledgling outfit, assisted by former Aberavon and Maesteg player Sean Holley, who left his post in charge of Gloucester's Academy to return home.

The team they were pulling together was an interesting mix of traditional Swansea flair and Neath steel. British & Irish Lions and Wales legend Scott Gibbs was handed the captaincy ahead of other experienced names like Gareth Llewellyn and Barry Williams, while there was a host of exciting young talent such as Gavin Henson, Shane Williams, Duncan and Adam Jones, and Jonathan Thomas.

There was also some recruitment, with a trio of players arriving from Bath: Swansea-born scrum-half Andy Williams, back row Gavin Thomas, and Samoan wing Elvis Seveali'i.

Behind the scenes, Swansea's Roger Blyth and Neath's Mike Cuddy were confirmed as the men to steer the ship through its maiden voyage as joint Chief Executives.

The playing strip was unveiled at the end of July to much criticism from the Swansea side of the support

Taking matchday advertising to new extremes

base, being predominantly black with white trim. The club logo featured Neath's Maltese Cross emblem, with an osprey superimposed across the top. Even though the change strip was the exact reverse and predominantly white, the fears from the St Helen's fan base that this was just Neath by another name were soon being voiced.

As the first season of regional rugby approached, the

Scott Gibbs leads the Ospreys out for their first ever Celtic League game, against Ulster at the Gnoll on 5 September 2003

what it was or who was behind it was forthcoming.

With tongues wagging as it to what these strange signs meant, it was eventually revealed that the 'mask' was an alternative logo for the new team based on the black eye strip of an osprey.

The 'big sell' of the start of a new era was no doubt hampered by the absence of the big name Welsh internationals, the players that supporters would want to leave their armchair to go and watch live, due to the forthcoming Rugby World Cup in Australia.

Nevertheless, despite being without six senior players, Ospreys management continued with their charm offensive in the build-up to their opening games, using every possible forum to speak directly to rugby fans in the area.

Warm-up matches against amateur opposition in Narberth, and Worcester from the English Premiership were positive, with the Ospreys winning both, 42–0 and 33–19 respectively.

The new regions would participate in an expanded Celtic League competition. Instead of being something of an afterthought, and a competition that simply filled the gaps between domestic league fixtures, the new-look Celtic League would, from the start of the 2003/04 season, become the sole professional league of the three participating countries, Ireland, Scotland and Wales.

The previous pool system with teams just playing each other once per season, either home or away, was replaced by a traditional home and away league format. This provided teams with a season-long, 22-round programme of matches, as well as a new knock-out competition, the Celtic Cup. In addition, the European

Ospreys undertook what was, as far as rugby in Wales was concerned, an unprecedented level of marketing activity in an attempt to engage the local community. The highlight was a guerrilla campaign that saw landmarks across the region being plastered with a 'mask' graphic, although originally no explanation as to

Cup, or the Heineken Cup as it was known, would provide additional cross-border competition.

The rugby map of Wales had been rewritten over the summer and as the first weekend of September approached, and with it the first round of fixtures for the new regions, nobody could accuse those at the coalface of Welsh rugby of meekly accepting their fate. They had instigated huge change, pushing it through in a matter of months, to ensure the long-term future of the game, they said.

No one would have been surprised if there were just a few nerves as the Ospreys prepared for their debut fixture in the Celtic League, versus Ulster at the Gnoll on Friday, 5th September, 2003.

Ospreys bosses declared themselves "satisfied" at season-ticket sales in the week leading up to the game, sales which had "exceeded expectation", while a crowd of 4,250 was present on that historic evening.

Whilst not the greatest crowd at a venue capable of holding in excess of 10,000, it was 58 per cent up on the recorded attendance when Swansea hosted Ulster the previous season (due to the structure of the competition that season, Neath hadn't played Ulster), so was certainly a positive start.

Those present were treated to a memorable evening. Dave Tiueti wrote his name into the history books, taking a pass off Scott Gibbs before haring through to touch down under the posts inside just two minutes to record the first Ospreys try in competitive action.

The hosts looked to build on that start, and were dominating territory, but a trio of classic counter attacks saw Ulster run in a hat-trick of tries from inside their own half, only three Shaun Connor penalties keeping

Dave Tiueti scores the Ospreys opening try just two minutes into the first game against Ulster

the new boys in touch at the break as they trailed by five points.

It was a swift start for the Ospreys once more after the break, Andy Williams providing the spark before Adrian Durston crossed to score, Connor converting to nudge his team ahead.

Connor then stretched the lead with his boot, a score which led to the first, tentative, shouts of 'Ospreys' ringing around the Gnoll. It would have been music to the ears of Blyth, Cuddy and their fellow directors.

Elvis Seveali'i then set up Gavin Henson for a third try and, although Ulster's Wallace put over three

A youthful Adam Jones goes on the charge but he can't stop the Ospreys going down to a fourth consecutive defeat, against Leinster at the end of November

French giants Toulouse come to Neath where they claim a comfortable 29–11 victory in the Heineken Cup

penalties, Ospreys nerves were settled late on when Gibbs sent Henson over for his second and the team's fourth try to secure a bonus point.

It ended 41–30, and by the final whistle the chants of 'Ospreys' were not so much tentative, as positively enthusiastic.

The Ospreys faced their first regional derby match a week later, away to the Newport Gwent Dragons side, and after the positivity of their opening fixture they were brought crashing back down to earth.

Unlike the Gnoll crowd the previous week, the home support at Rodney Parade made it clear that their loyalties remained with Newport ahead of Gwent, their chants as the home team emerged before kick-off not leaving any room for ambiguity.

Once the action got underway, it was a physical,

Springbok Stefan Terblanche gets a close-up view of Gavin Henson in action as the Ospreys claim a first European win, at the sixth attempt

low-quality and bad-tempered affair, the Dragons taking advantage of the Ospreys having Scott Gibbs and Gavin Thomas yellow carded to win 29–19.

The region's first ever Celtic Cup campaign was a short lived one, Henson and Seveali'i scoring tries as they crashed out at the first round stage, losing 35–21 away to Leinster, ill-discipline again proving costly as Lyndon Bateman and Steve Tandy both spent time in the sin-bin.

St Helen's then played host to its first ever Ospreys game at the end of September and more than 5,200 turned up to watch their new region overcome Munster 33–26. A kicking masterclass from Gavin Henson saw him clock up 18 points, with tries coming from James Storey, Dave Tiueti and Andy Williams.

With two wins from the first three league fixtures, the signs for the Ospreys were promising. The next opponents, at the start of October, were the Celtic Warriors, the Bridgend and Pontypridd amalgamation. It was a relationship that was already showing signs of hitting the buffers, with Ponty facing administration and the Union standing by to step in.

Nevertheless, the Warriors boasted an enviable squad, regardless of Rugby World Cup absentees, so Lyn Jones and his men knew it wouldn't be easy when they travelled to the Brewery Field.

Winger Gareth Morris, making his first regional start, caught the eye with a brace of tries for the Ospreys, but it was 21-year-old Henson – inexplicably left out of Wales' squad for Australia – who stole the show once more, kicking 22 points and creating Morris' first score to guide the Ospreys to a 32–22 win.

Henson was the star man again a week later as he helped himself to another 22-point haul, all with his boot, as he inspired his team to a 42–18 win over Edinburgh at the Gnoll. With tries coming from Scott Gibbs, Shaun Connor, Andy Newman and James Storey, the bonus-point win allowed the fledgling Ospreys to overtake their opponents and climb to the top of the Celtic League table for the first time.

It had been a dream start for the new entity, and with a stated ambition to not only be the best performing regional side in Wales, but also the most professional, the appointment of Andrew Donald as Chief Executive was announced. Donald was to be responsible for day-to-day activity at the Ospreys, reporting to Blyth and Cuddy who now became joint Managing Directors.

It was, said the Ospreys, the first time a Welsh club or region had appointed such a post purely on commercial expertise and would allow the region to make bigger strides off the field.

As promising as that sounded, the new Chief Executive had no on-field influence, and he would have watched on in dismay as the Ospreys were knocked off their perch at the top of the table in astonishing fashion, thumped 43–6 by Cardiff Blues on their first visit to the Arms Park, Blues wing Lee Abdul scoring four of his team's six tries.

Alarming for all Welsh rugby people was the fact that such a big derby match could attract a crowd of just 3,500. Despite some encouraging signs, regional rugby was still struggling to take hold. With Pontypridd relinquishing its stake in the Celtic Warriors following administration, and financial difficulties at Rodney Parade seeing the Dragons also going into administration, the transition certainly wasn't proving easy.

Connacht then left St Helen's with a maximum five-point haul, taking advantage of a weakened Ospreys pack to win 33–22, Rhodri Wells scoring the host's only try.

After such a fine start to the campaign the Ospreys had seemingly lost their way, going down to a third straight defeat at the hands of Borders at the start of November, 22–16.

*

The League went into a three-week break to avoid clashing with the knockout stages of the Rugby World Cup on the other side of the world, and when the action resumed again at the end of November, the Ospreys were strengthened not only by their international contingent, after Wales went out to England in the quarter-finals, but by a world-class addition to the squad that made observers sit up and take notice.

South African Test star Stefan Terblanche, with 19 tries in 37 internationals, joined the region on an initial

Along with Gavin Thomas, veteran Welsh international Gareth Llewellyn was transfer listed at the end of January

Andy Lloyd soars high to claim the ball as St Helen's hosts its first Ospreys v Scarlets derby

Andrew Millward, Barry Williams and Paul James — a classic front-row combination that went on to make almost 400 Osprey appearances between them.

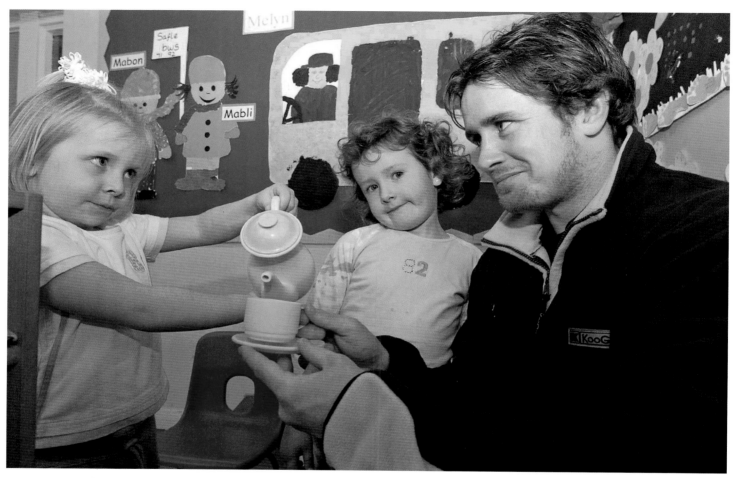

Shane Williams enjoys a tea break with some young admirers

18-month contract and would arrive in south Wales at the end of November.

Even with their internationals back in the fold, the Ospreys were unable to halt their slump, a classy Leinster scoring six tries in a 36–25 win at the Gnoll where only 18 points from Henson's boot kept them in touch.

Four straight losses wasn't the preparation that Lyn Jones would've wanted ahead of the Ospreys' first ever Heineken Cup campaign.

Elvis Seveali'i and Shaun Connor spend time with local younsgters

Terblanche in tow for his Ospreys debut, and with Jones backing his squad to make an impression.

However, they were forced to endure a tough afternoon. Shane Williams scored the region's first ever try in the elite European competition and Scott Gibbs added a second, but the game finished 29–20 to the home team.

A week later the Ospreys hosted Edinburgh at St Helen's, a team they had already sent packing once that season. However, in appalling conditions in Swansea, a disappointing crowd of just 1,822 watched the Scots return home with a winning bonus point after a 32–16 victory to leave the region's hopes of reaching the knockout stages hanging on a thread just two games in.

There was a first regional era clash with the Scarlets over the New Year period, with a bumper 10,195 crowd present at Stradey to see an improved Ospreys push the hosts all the way, trailing 18–15 with 70 minutes gone, only for two late tries to ensure a 28–15 bonus-point win for the hosts.

It was then back to the Heineken Cup and the daunting challenge of back-to-back games against French giants Toulouse. True to form, the Ospreys came off second best, losing 29–6 in France, before a 29–11 reverse at the Gnoll.

Just days after that loss, the ninth in a row, and ahead of the next Heineken Cup game in Edinburgh, came the surprise announcement that captain Scott Gibbs was retiring from rugby. The 33-year-old, who had scored four tries in 15 regional appearances, cited the heavy travelling of the Celtic League as a reason, saying that it made it difficult for him to combine rugby with his burgeoning business career:

The Ospreys had been drawn in a pool with reigning champions Toulouse, Leeds Tykes from the Zurich Premiership in England, and Celtic League rivals Edinburgh.

First up was an away day in Yorkshire, with winger

What I had not fully appreciated when accepting a two-year contract with the Ospreys was the effect of all the extra travelling now that the Celtic League is played home and away. I have been out of the country for long periods and that has put a strain on my work. It got to the stage where I was being stretched, with neither the company nor the Ospreys getting my best. I was delegating at work and missing training sessions. Something had to give. I told the Ospreys what was on my mind a couple of months ago.

Minus the skipper, the barren run continued as Edinburgh ran in four tries to inflict a tenth straight defeat on the Ospreys, who were still to claim their first point in the competition after a 33–15 defeat in their fifth game.

The old saying goes that the darkest hour is just before dawn, and so it was to prove for Ospreys fans. With just 2,000 present at St Helen's the following week, an Andy Williams try was enough to ensure the region avoided a Heineken Cup whitewash, winning 10–3 against Leeds in the final round. There was a debut for Andy Lloyd in that game, a young back five forward who had signed for his home region from Bath in December.

Assistant Coach, Sean Holley, was a relieved man as he paid tribute to the spirit of the team: "I was delighted with the character the side showed. We've been through a tough period but we believe in what we are about here and what we are trying to do. Nobody said it would be easy but we are pulling together as a unit and I genuinely believe that this organisation can go places given time."

The win, on the last day of January, ended a run of defeats that stretched back to mid-October.

Just 72 hours later came another announcement from the Ospreys of players leaving. International forwards Gareth Llewellyn and Gavin Thomas, who both missed the win over Leeds, had been transfer listed and were free to find themselves new clubs. Thomas had featured 15 times for the Ospreys while Llewellyn had six appearances to his credit since returning from the Rugby World Cup.

Managing Director, Roger Blyth, explained that, "We are in a process which amounts to a redefining of the squad… the full weight of the management team and the board will be behind Lyn Jones as the necessary changes are now made to keep the team moving forwards."

The redefining of the squad following a troubled few months for the region was extended to the management team the following day when Team Manager, Byron Mugford, parted company with the organisation.

However, despite the ongoing turmoil, the win over Leeds to end the barren run had lifted spirits noticeably and it was backed up by a 33–11 win over Glasgow at the Gnoll at the start of February.

The following weekend saw Scott Gibbs make one final appearance in an Ospreys shirt, turning out in midfield to help strengthen an injury-hit team that faced a tough challenge away to league leaders Ulster. It came as no surprise that a weakened team found themselves trailing by 24–0 inside 25 minutes but they stuck to the task to add respectability to the score line, eventually going down 31–19.

In a complete turnaround of the mid-winter form, the Ospreys then embarked on a five-match winning run.

The Dragons were seen off 26–14, before what was to be a landmark win for the region, an 18–15 victory in Munster thanks to two tries from Elvis Seveali'i, a result that Lyn Jones declared "... a huge step forward for us".

Celtic Warriors were beaten 23–11 at the Gnoll before an incredible finish in Edinburgh saw the Ospreys gain revenge for their Heineken Cup defeats to the Scottish side, late tries from Andrew Millward and Richie Pugh securing a 35–31 victory. Next, Cardiff Blues were beaten 34–13 at St Helen's at the end of March.

The behind the scenes changes continued with the introduction of former Wales second row, Derwyn Jones, to the set-up. He left Cardiff Blues to take up the post of Regional Rugby Manager, overseeing rugby activity following the departure of the Team Manager two months earlier.

The final weeks of the season saw the Ospreys struggle to maintain the intensity they had shown throughout February and March and results were generally disappointing.

There was a 24–21 loss in Connacht, the Irish side overturning an 18–7 half-time deficit, before Borders were smashed 60–7 at the Gnoll as the Ospreys ran in nine tries. Gavin Henson scored three of them, in a personal 30-point haul, while Shane Williams grabbed a pair with Andy Williams, Elvis Seveali'i, Stefan Terblanche and Jonathan Thomas also scoring.

An uninspiring 16-all draw away to Leinster was followed by an 18–15 home defeat to champions elect the Scarlets on the penultimate weekend of the season.

The season drew to a surprisingly exciting climax as the Ospreys were involved in a thrilling contest away to Glasgow; both teams scoring four tries in a 34–31 home win.

Jonathan Thomas, Andy Newman, Richie Pugh and then Duncan Jones with the last play of the match, ensured that the Ospreys secured the two match points they needed to finish above Cardiff Blues in fifth place to grab the final Heineken Cup spot, with the Blues, as worst placed Welsh team, condemned to the second tier competition, the Challenge Cup.

However, events over the coming weeks would mean that the Welsh rugby map would change again, and that change would mean that the Blues would join the Ospreys, the Scarlets and the Dragons in the Heineken Cup at the expense of the Celtic Warriors.

2

The Ospreys inaugural season had certainly been a tumultuous one.

Described by BBC Wales in their preview of the forthcoming campaign as 'shambolic', things had certainly improved in the latter part of the season, following the mid-term nadir of ten straight losses and the departure of some senior squad members.

Form had improved in the second half of the season though, giving hope for those who had got on board from the early days that Neath-Swansea Ospreys could possibly have a bright future.

However, the summer of 2004 once more saw Welsh rugby in a state of flux as regional rugby, just one year old, again stood on the brink.

Celtic Warriors, the region formed a little more than twelve months earlier from a merger of Pontypridd and Bridgend to represent the Mid Glamorgan and South Powys area, had failed to establish themselves off the field despite acquitting themselves well on it, finishing the season in fourth place ahead of both the Ospreys and Cardiff Blues.

Financial problems at Pontypridd led to the sale of their 50 per cent shareholding to Bridgend owner Leighton Samuel. Samuel then reneged on an agreement to share games between Bridgend's Brewery Field home and Sardis Road, Pontypridd's ground, opting to play all home matches at Bridgend.

With attendances falling, at the end of the season Samuel accepted an offer from the WRU to purchase Bridgend's shareholding after Cardiff had rejected the offer to merge with the Warriors. Although Samuel was to later change his mind, the transaction was considered legally binding and on 1 June 2004, the WRU liquidated the Warriors.

With Welsh rugby now reduced to just four regions it meant there was an entire squad of players, not to mention a coaching team and backroom staff, looking for alternative employment. There were also supporters, who had already been forced to embrace massive change just a year ago, left with no team to support.

Chief Executive, Andrew Donald, made it clear that the Ospreys would do what they could to help both players and fans, saying:

> The Ospreys will try to help by absorbing as many of the Warriors players into the current Ospreys squad that we can, absorbing players' contracts wherever and whenever possible. And, if there is the will from supporters, we will move heaven and earth to bring in as much of the Warriors' region within the Ospreys set-up as we possibly can, but only if fans want us to do so.

Looking sharp at the start of the new campaign

Following the demise of the Warriors, the Ospreys were quick to snap up a number of players, providing greater depth to their squad.

Experience came in the form of physical Australian-born Wales second row Brent Cockbain, while another Wales international, centre Sonny Parker, arrived shortly after. Some highly promising youngsters also made the switch including the much sought after back row Ryan Jones, centre David Bishop and wing Richard Mustoe.

A third Welsh international, 32-year-old hooker Mefin Davies, was left in the difficult position of not finding a full-time contract after having his Warriors contract ripped up, and he signed for Neath, but would also step up to represent the Ospreys in the first half of the season before crossing Offa's Dyke to join Gloucester in December. A number of back-room staff also made the switch.

With the addition of Kiwi scrum-half Jason Spice from Wellington Hurricanes and the in-demand Shane Williams rejecting offers from French clubs Béziers and Castres to sign a new three-year deal with the Ospreys, there was a far more stable look to the regional set-up ahead of the new campaign.

Indeed, as Chairman Mike James mused, facilities under construction including a new stadium in Swansea and a state-of-the-art training venue in Llandarcy would not only "be the envy of every other regional rugby side in Wales", they would "indelibly mark the approach the Ospreys are now taking in ensuring the advent of European and world-class rugby in the region."

Furthermore, he added, "The Ospreys are now in a prime position to carve out a piece of rugby history. Our intention is to see the Ospreys take regional rugby to a new level, delivering the very essence of community-driven regional rugby, for the ultimate benefit of Welsh rugby and the national team."

It was a bold statement of ambition from the Ospreys, but the bullishness in the boardroom was more than matched on the training paddock as Rugby Manager, Derwyn Jones, declared that the region was targeting the last eight in Europe despite winning just one in six last time out. The Ospreys were pooled with Castres, Harlequins and Celtic League rivals Munster, a tough draw by anyone's standards, but Jones said: "Making the quarters is an achievable goal. Obviously it will be difficult as the competition is so strong, but I hope the fans will get behind us."

Before the team could think about the Heineken Cup, or even the Celtic League for that matter, they had to get through a couple of tough warm-up games in August.

First, they travelled to the south of France, to Bagnères in Midi-Pyrenees, for a training week that would be rounded off with a difficult game against Toulouse, European champions in 1996 and 2003 and who had emerged from the Ospreys' group in the previous season to finish runners-up to London Wasps just a couple of months earlier.

The demise of Celtic Warriors was even felt in Bagnères, as the Ospreys found themselves up against Toulouse's new signing and former Warriors star, Welsh international Gareth Thomas, who featured at full-back for the French side.

Early tries from Vincent Clerc and Yannick Bru had given Toulouse the advantage but the Ospreys rallied well as back row Nathan Bonner-Evans and Ryan Jones scored to narrow the gap to just two points.

However, Toulouse sub Jean-François Montauriol had a huge impact, the flanker scoring two second-half tries as his side came out on top 28–14.

Bath came to St Helen's two weeks later for what proved to be a full-blooded affair belying the pre-season friendly billing, in front of a promising crowd of almost 5,000. A Richie Pugh try gave the Ospreys an early lead but they were unable to add any further points as Bath won 15–5.

Post-Warriors break-up, the Ospreys had agreed to embrace the Bridgend area into the regional set-up, but the harsh reality of the fixture schedule for the new season saw all home games divided equally between the Gnoll and St Helen's. As Andrew Donald explained:

> While seeming like a great idea on the surface, the reality of actually staging a game at Bridgend is fraught with difficulties. Aside from logistical problems... we are aware that the move could actually alienate three sets of supporters rather than embrace supporters with a true sense of inclusiveness. We have a great deal of work to do in the Bridgend area over the next season and in the run-up to Morfa.

And so it was that the opening day of the Celtic League season saw the Ospreys return to St Helen's to entertain Munster.

Ryan Jones on his debut for the Ospreys after switching from the now defunct fifth region, Celtic Warriors

Sonny Parker also settled quickly after making the move to the Ospreys

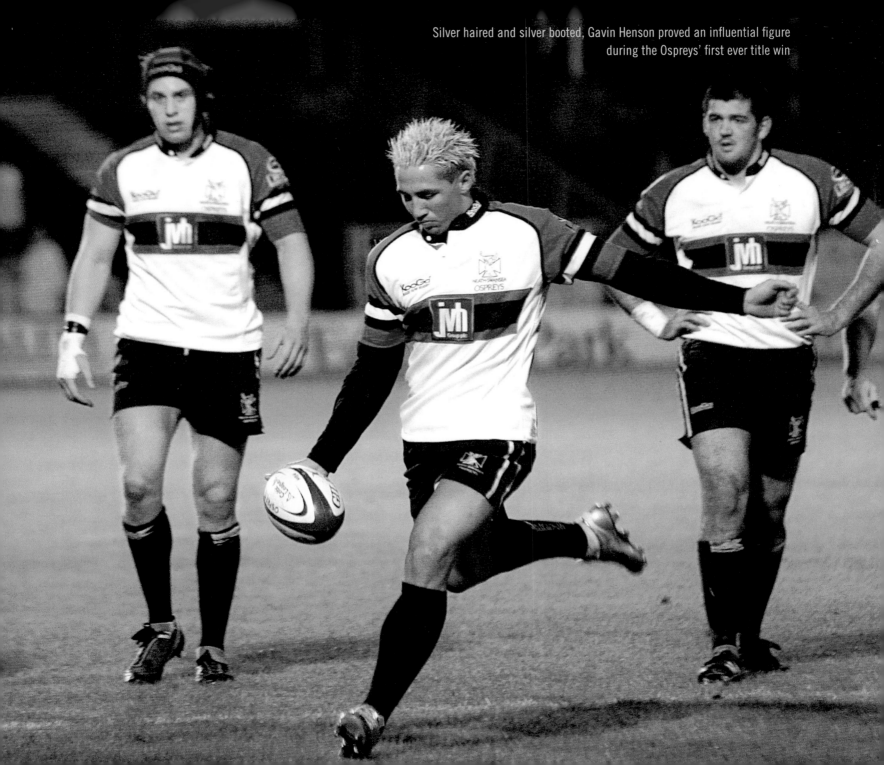

Silver haired and silver booted, Gavin Henson proved an influential figure
during the Ospreys' first ever title win

Shane Williams celebrates one of his two tries as the Ospreys defeat the Scarlets on Boxing Day

The hosts got off to a flying start as tries from new boys Spice and Bishop allowed them to build up a 20–0 half-time lead, Gavin Henson kicking ten points. Munster rallied in the third quarter, a brace from former All Black Christian Cullen helping them cut the deficit to just three points. The Ospreys refused to panic though, and with 79 minutes gone Adrian Durston got his team's third try. Incredibly, there was still time for them to claim a fourth, and with it a bonus point, as second row Lyndon Bateman crashed over to round off a 34–17 win.

It was the perfect start to the season, and next up

were back-to-back derbies against the Scarlets and the Blues.

The fine start to the season continued with two good wins against their Welsh rivals. The first was a Gavin Henson inspired win, the full-back scoring 18 points including a length of the field run to touch down under the posts, with Richie Pugh also scoring a try as the Ospreys romped home 23–6 against the champions at Stradey Park.

A week later it was even more impressive as they thumped the Blues at the Gnoll, Duncan Jones, David Bishop, Jason Spice, Sonny Parker and Henson all touching down in a 39–3 win.

The winning run continued as a rampant Ospreys side highlighted that they would be a force to be reckoned with this season. Another bonus-point win followed on the road, as Ulster were defeated 37–24 in Belfast before Glasgow suffered the same fate at the Gnoll on the first weekend of October, the Ospreys running in six tries in a 40–17 win over Glasgow.

Gavin Henson was proving increasingly influential to the Ospreys game, his reliable kicking and ability to run it back from deep constantly putting the Ospreys on the front foot in the early weeks of the season, and he had helped himself to 78 points in the first five games.

He duly added another 13 in an edgy 23–15 away win against Borders, Ryan Jones and Andy Newman scoring a try apiece.

The Ospreys went into the final game before the Celtic League broke for European competition boasting a 100 per cent record from six matches. Game seven was a top of the table clash with Leinster in Swansea. Skipper Barry Williams was confident going into the game, praising the progress his region had made since the end of the previous season: "We made some good signings over the summer and are a team full of confidence," he said.

It was to prove a tight and tense affair, with little between the two sides. The home team dominated territory, but the lead was just 6–3 inside the final ten minutes. However, with Leinster a man short following a yellow card to David Holwell, the Ospreys were able to take advantage, Adrian Durston sending over Sonny Parker for the clincher.

Lyn Jones was beaming with pride post-match as he hailed his team's performance, claiming it was evidence that the controversial switch to regional rugby was paying off: "That was exactly the sort of win we wanted, and we deserved it. It was a huge challenge, an intense game against a very strong pack. Two years ago not one Welsh club would have beaten that Leinster team but now we've got the back-up that the Irish regional sides have had for years."

With seven straight wins in the Celtic League the Ospreys were belatedly taking flight, but the Heineken Cup was an altogether different kind of challenge.

First up was a daunting trip to France, where just one Welsh team had ever won in European competition, to face Castres. Although they traveled with confidence, they knew it was likely to be tough and that was exactly how it proved to be as the French side blew them away.

Castres were 23–7 up by half-time, with an Adam Jones try after good work by Andy Lloyd, converted by Henson, all the Ospreys had to show for their efforts. The hosts maintained the pressure after the break, eventually claiming a bonus point, meaning a late Jason

Spice score was just adding a gloss of respectability as it finished 38–17. Jonathan Thomas was red carded for a punch in the final minute, an act that would lead to an 18-day ban.

Spice denied suggestions post-match that despite their fine league form his team were not ready for the step-up in intensity that comes with the Heineken Cup, saying: "We knew what we were in for, came here with high expectations. We just didn't play well and made too many mistakes."

There was an opportunity for the Ospreys to bounce back a week later when Celtic rivals Munster came to the Gnoll. A bumper crowd of more than 10,000, the first sell-out at the Neath ground in ten years, were treated to a pulsating spectacle that remained in the balance until the final whistle.

Ultimately though, six penalties from Henson were not enough, a Peter Stringer try the difference as Munster clung on to win 20–18. The Ospreys may have had a perfect record in the Celtic League but they were zero from two in the Heineken.

The fallout from the match saw winger Richard Mustoe cited for stamping on Munster prop Marcus Horan, after the Irish international was left covered in blood from a head wound. A disciplinary panel found Mustoe guilty and banned him for twelve weeks.

The back-to-back defeats left the Ospreys with something of a hangover as they returned to Celtic League action in November, minus ten players named in Mike Ruddock's Wales squad for the autumn internationals.

They suffered the first league defeat of the season in a Welsh derby against the Dragons at Rodney Parade, having to settle for a losing bonus point thanks to a late Dave Tiueti try to leave it 33–29 to the hosts at the whistle.

Tries from Andy Newman, Stefan Terblanche and Aled Brew then secured a 31–15 win away to Edinburgh, but November ended with a second league defeat of the season, Connacht grabbing an unlikely 10–9 win at the Gnoll after young outside half Matthew Jones had endured a miserable evening with the boot, missing four kicks that would have handed the Ospreys a comfortable win.

The start of December saw the announcement that Chief Executive, Andrew

Shaun Connor helps the Ospreys to a convincing win over Borders while the international contingent are away on Six Nations duty

Lyndon Bateman soars high to claim the ball against the Dragons at St Helen's

Donald, was stepping down, with his responsibilities being divided between joint Managing Directors' Mike Cuddy and Roger Blyth.

Harlequins came to St Helen's for the first game of a European double-header, the Ospreys looking for a belated first win of their Heineken Cup campaign against a team sitting rock bottom in the Zurich Premiership.

They got off to a disastrous start, conceding a try inside the first minute, but the hosts then dominated territory and four Gavin Henson penalties in each half saw the Ospreys home to a comfortable 24–7 win.

The following weekend saw the Ospreys travel to the Twickenham Stoop, where an impressive six-try demolition of the Quins kept them in with a chance of achieving their goal of a quarter-final spot.

It was Henson who once again pulled the strings, helping himself to a 26-point haul including a try in each half. The other tries came from Ryan Jones, Shane Williams, Matthew Jones and Stefan Terblanche, with England centre Will Greenwood scoring the solitary Harlequins touchdown as it finished 46–19.

A pre-Christmas 13–9 Celtic League defeat to Munster in Cork kept Ospreys' feet firmly on the ground before a festive derby double-header that saw the region extend its lead at the top of the table.

More than 10,000 packed into the Gnoll on Boxing Day to watch the hosts record a bonus-point win over the Scarlets, tries from Shane Williams (2), Barry Williams and James Bater helping the Ospreys to a 28–7 win that left Scarlets Director of Rugby, Gareth Jenkins, hailing the "individual brilliance" of fans' favourite Shane.

A 15–9 New Year's Day win at Cardiff Arms Park over the Blues, with tries from Pugh and Spice, then set the Ospreys up nicely for a crunch Heineken Cup clash against Munster in Limerick. Assistant Coach, Sean Holley recognised the size of the challenge that lay ahead: "It will be the biggest game of our season because it's make-or-break in terms of our Heineken Cup campaign. The result will tell us whether the final match against Castres is a meaningful game or not."

The answer, unfortunately, was to be 'not', as Munster maintained their unbeaten European record at Thomond Park with a hard earned 20–10 win which meant the Ospreys welcomed Castres, who were still hopeful of progressing, to the Gnoll for a game where they were playing for little more than pride.

As it was, they put in possibly their best performance of the campaign, tries from Richie Rees and Elvis Seveali'i helping them to a 20–11 win, which meant Munster won the pool and Castres missed out on even a best runner-up spot.

The Ospreys had failed to achieve their quarter-final target, but with three wins and two competitive defeats to Munster, there was plenty to be pleased about, the

Jason Spice runs in one of his two scores in the 30-0 hammering of the Dragons

defeat in Castres the only real black mark as Holley acknowledged after the final game:

We are still a young organisation less than two years old, albeit one with high expectations. We want to be at the top table of the European game and I think we've made big strides throughout this campaign. We've made people sit up and take notice of us. Although we are going out at the pool stage, we've said all week that next year's campaign started with this campaign. If we can replicate the kind of performance we've put on today, then we can be optimistic about our chances next season.

Skipper Barry Williams (bottom left) lays down the law to his forwards

As Wales coach Mike Ruddock named seven Ospreys in his Six Nations squad, the region was able to tighten its grip on top spot in the Celtic League with the narrowest of wins over Ulster at St Helen's. Gavin Henson scored all the points in a contest where the lead changed hands several times, the full-back needing to slot over an injury time penalty to win it, 22–21.

A 27–27 draw with Glasgow away from home kept things ticking over, a late try from Stefan Terblanche, converted by Matthew Jones, securing a share of the spoils. With Munster losing away to the Scarlets, it meant that the Ospreys extended their lead over the Irish side to seven points.

While Wales were getting their Six Nations campaign off to an impressive start with wins over England and Italy, the Ospreys continued what was beginning to look like an unstoppable charge to the title with another bonus-point win at the Gnoll, 34–10 over Borders.

There were just four league games remaining, the first of those against third placed Leinster, one of two teams that retained some hope of catching the Ospreys. However, a 16–12 win at Donnybrook allowed the region to open up what was looking like an unassailable 12-point lead over second placed Munster, that left their Irish rivals praying for an unlikely slump from the Ospreys which would mean them failing to win any of their remaining three games (they'd just lost three in 17 Celtic League games to date).

Newport Gwent Dragons were next, with the Ospreys knowing that if they won and Munster, who were playing Ulster at home, failed to secure a point, then they would be crowned champions.

It was one-way traffic at St Helen's as they destroyed their Welsh rivals 30–0, tries from Richard Mustoe, Adrian Durston and Jason Spice (2) securing the full five points, but a Munster victory also meaning the champagne stayed on ice.

Despite the convincing win there was no pleasing Lyn Jones though, who declared: "We didn't play well but I'm relieved that we got the win."

Wins for Wales over France, Scotland and Ireland meant that the national team had won their first Grand Slam in 27 years, and the Ospreys' international contingent returned to help the final push towards what would be an historic first league crown for a rugby entity that was still to celebrate the end of its second year.

At the end of March Munster kept their slim title hopes alive with a 24–8 win over the Dragons, but the following night it was all about the Ospreys as another capacity crowd filled the Gnoll in anticipation of a win that would secure the league crown and kick-off a title party.

On a damp Neath evening, the Ospreys were always in front as they eased their way to victory over Edinburgh. Gavin Henson was again to the fore as he scored 24 points in a 29–12 success after Jason Spice had grabbed the opening try, taking Steve Tandy's scoring pass to go over in the corner.

Henson grabbed a second-half try after a long floating pass from Adam Jones, before what seemed like the entire crowd spilled on to the pitch at the final whistle to celebrate.

It was a stunning title success, one that no observers had predicted at the start of the season and underlined the enormous potential of the Ospreys.

With a league crown under their belt, an improved showing in Europe, and three capacity 10,280 crowds during the season, the move to a new home on the banks of the River Tawe couldn't have been better timed.

Reflecting on the achievement, Lyn Jones said: "Winning the Celtic League is reward for this side being the best team in the competition. It's a fantastic feeling, it's been a lot of hard work and I'm delighted to see so many good players fulfilling their potential. Now we can look forward to moving onto bigger and better things."

Barry Wiliams lifts the Celtic League trophy at the Gnoll in front of his team-mates

Barry Williams wrote his place in the history books as the first Ospreys captain to lift silverware, an achievement he says will live with him forever. Speaking several years later on the region's website, he said:

I'll never, ever forget that night. For me as captain it was a really special moment, lifting the Celtic League trophy was something that will always mean so much to me. I remember the team talk in the dressing room before the match, and me telling the guys that we were going to go down in history as the first ever Ospreys team to win anything. There's a picture of me lifting the trophy in front of the team, I remember the exact moment perfectly. I think there were 11,000 supporters at the Gnoll that night and every one of them was on the pitch with the team as I was presented with the trophy. It was a great experience. Being the first captain of the region to lift a trophy is something that no-one will ever take away from me. It had been a hard time for everybody involved with the region, but we had belief in what we

Stefan Terblanche with the silverware as crowds flood onto the Gnoll pitch

were doing and the night that we beat Edinburgh to clinch the league title was the moment when the penny dropped as to what we could achieve at the Ospreys.

With the league title secured two weeks before the end of the season, the Ospreys could relax and enjoy their final fixture, a trip to Galway to face Connacht. They made light work of the challenge, scoring all their points in a 22–13 victory in the first half through tries from that man Henson, Jonathan Thomas and Shane

Williams, Henson adding seven with his boot also.

The format of the season, with an odd number of teams competing due to the demise of the Celtic Warriors, even gave the Ospreys the luxury of sitting out the final weekend – although whether Lyn Jones and his team would have considered it a luxury had the title been hanging on the final round of fixtures was anybody's guess.

It has been an incredible and memorable season for

Barry Williams celebrates the Ospreys' first ever league title

the region but it wasn't over yet, as the Celtic Cup, in a new format for its second and final season, was still up for grabs, played for between the top eight teams in the league.

Ulster were seen off 23–16 at St Helen's to secure a place in the last four, but defeat at Stradey Park to the Scarlets, 23–15, ended Ospreys interests.

What it didn't do though was take the gloss off the Ospreys' first league title, a success that whetted the appetite for the first season at the region's new home in SA1.

3

There is no doubt that 2005 was a landmark year for the Ospreys, one that saw the regional concept truly take hold for the first time across South-West Wales.

Of course, the region's first ever silverware was perfectly timed. However, there were other significant factors ahead of the new season that really helped to take Ospreys rugby on to another level.

After two years of ground-sharing, playing at the run-down outdated homes of Neath and Swansea RFCs, the Ospreys would have a new home for the forthcoming season – and what a home.

The £27million, 20,520 capacity venue at Morfa in Landore, which would become known as the Liberty Stadium, was a state of the art ground to rival any in Europe, and would be jointly shared by the Ospreys and Swansea City FC.

A breathtaking stadium with spectacular views from every seat, the move would bring with it its own challenge – namely how to fill a ground with a capacity more than four times the previous season's average crowd!

A first step towards achieving that goal saw the significant announcement over the summer that the prefix 'Neath-Swansea' was being dropped to reflect the fact that the Ospreys no longer represented just two historic old clubs, but a far wider geographic area incorporating the Bridgend district too.

With a trophy in the cabinet, a name change and a new home, it meant that the Ospreys were no longer weighed down by history and were ready to take flight.

Built on the site of the former Morfa Athletics Stadium and playing fields, the Liberty had been many years in the making – well before the inception of the Ospreys – and finally became reality that summer. To open it, English giants London Wasps, the reigning Premiership champions, were invited to Swansea for a cross-border 'battle of Britain' challenge match at the end of August.

There was also a new training base for the players when they reported back after their summer breaks, with the Llandarcy Academy of Sport open for business and giving the Ospreys a day-to-day HQ to match their new stadium.

Befitting of a growing organisation that now boasted facilities the envy of the rugby world, there was also the pre-season announcement of a lucrative shirt sponsorship deal which would see energy company npower renewables' logo on the front of the shirt.

Team strengthening was minimal ahead of the new season, with Swansea-born winger Jonny Vaughton

New season, new era for the Ospreys

signing from Cardiff Blues and former Scarlets captain Leigh Davies, a centre, the only arrivals.

Heading in the opposite direction were three overseas players who had given sterling service to the region in its first two seasons, all of whom played in the first ever competitive fixture at the Gnoll versus Ulster in 2003.

Canadian second row, Luke Tait, Samoan winger Elvis Seveali'i and Tongan centre, Dave Tiueti had, between them, clocked up well over 100 appearances in just two seasons, with Tiueti forever etched in Ospreys history after scoring the first ever try in a competitive fixture for the region in their debut win over Ulster.

Another significant addition to the Ospreys' ranks was former Wales captain Jonathan Humphreys, appointed as Forwards Coach after retiring from playing at the end of the previous season.

The Ospreys had just the one fixture ahead of the new campaign, Lyn Jones brushing aside suggestions that his team would start the season undercooked after five of his players had returned late to training following a disastrous summer with the Lions in New Zealand (a tour where Ospreys youngster Ryan Jones was universally acclaimed as possibly the only Lion to have enhanced his reputation), with a further eight having toured North America with Wales.

Head Coach Jones said: "We work with the team day-in, day out, and we know what we need to do to get them up and running for the first game and beyond.

Pre-match entertainment ahead of the first ever Ospreys match at the Liberty Stadium

They've had a long year and we don't want them tired out before the season even gets underway. We'll be ready."

And so it was Wasps, who had won the English title three years in a row, who provided the opposition for the Ospreys, themselves reigning Celtic champions, in the first ever rugby fixture at the Liberty.

Incredibly for a team which, despite winning the league the previous season had struggled to reach 6,000 spectators for long periods of the campaign, more than 18,000 turned out to welcome the Ospreys into their new home, a clear sign of the potential that the new venue would allow the region to tap into.

On a historic evening where many present were attending their first ever Ospreys match, fans were treated to a spectacular opening ceremony, a combination of high adrenaline music, theatre and circus with real fire special effects and a giant heliosphere. Headlining the ceremony was a performance by Welsh singing star Charlotte Church, adding a touch of glamour to proceedings.

There wasn't a fairy tale ending to proceeding though as the visitors spoilt the party, claiming an 18–10 win despite early Ospreys tries from Stefan Terblanche (the first at the Liberty Stadium) and an up and coming youngster by the name of Alun Wyn Jones who was being tipped for a bright future.

David Moffett hailed the evening as "the dawning of a new era in professionalism in Wales".

The pleasing news that season-ticket sales had

trebled to more than 4,500 was a further boost, the Liberty factor already having a positive impact on Ospreys finances.

The following weekend saw the Ospreys back at the Liberty for the first game of their title defence; Leinster the visitors as another five-figure crowd packed in to cheer on their region.

They didn't have to wait long before they were on their feet celebrating as another young talent, by the name of Andrew Bishop, crashed over under the posts to score the first try inside 20 seconds. A try from skipper Barry Williams then allowed the Ospreys to take a five-point lead at the break, and in a game of nip and tuck with the lead changing hands several times in the second half, Bishop touched down once again before a late penalty from Matthew Jones allowed the Ospreys to claim the spoils with a 22–20 win.

The feel-good factor was blown away a week later though when the Ospreys found themselves on the wrong end of a 37–10 thumping by Munster at Cork's Musgrave Park. If possible with such a score line, it was a result that flattered the Ospreys somewhat as Munster grabbed a bonus point and led by 34 points going into the final minute. Only a late Barry Williams try, converted by Matthew Jones, added the slightest touch of respectability to the score line.

A 15–9 win over the Dragons at the Liberty four days later was then followed by consecutive defeats in Scotland, 16–6 at Borders and 24–18 versus Edinburgh, which meant that the champions already appeared to be on the ropes having lost as many league games by the end of September (three) as they had during the entire 2004/05 season.

The Ospreys sent for reinforcements in the form of a pair of New Zealanders. Goal-kicking full-back Adrian Cashmore, a twice-capped All Black from Waikato Chiefs, and NZ sevens' star Damian Karauna, a utility player capable of operating across the back-line, would increase the options available behind the scrum.

Alun Wyn Jones celebrates scoring for the Ospreys during the opening game at the Liberty Stadium

After the disappointing start to their title defence, there was a distraction from the league the following weekend as the Ospreys featured for the first time in the Anglo-Welsh Powergen Cup. New for this season, it pitted together the four Welsh regions and the twelve teams from the top division in England, with a big day out in Twickenham for the final in April.

The Ospreys were drawn to face three West Country teams, with a trip to Gloucester first up. They were trailing within two minutes through a James Simpson-Daniel try, and although Steve Tandy replied, it was Gloucester who led 13–7 at the break. The hosts pulled away in the second half though, a late try from Henry Paul sealing a 23–7 win at Kingsholm.

Bath came to the Liberty a week later, with the Ospreys knowing that only a win would keep alive their interests in the competition. When Matthew Jones converted his own try on 47 minutes, following a first-half penalty try, they seemed on course to do just that. However, Bath hit back with former Osprey Andy Williams, who had returned to his former club following the arrival of Jason Spice, at the fore with a try as the guests eventually won 27–20.

The Heineken Cup was looming large, and with it the unenviable challenge of facing up to a pair of French giants in Stade Français and Clermont Auvergne, along with the small matter of twice winners, Leicester Tigers.

First though, after four straight losses there was a chance to try and play themselves back into form when Connacht visited the Liberty Stadium. It was the Ospreys who came out on top in a poor game, 18–17, but it was a win dipped in a huge dose of controversy.

The losing run had seemed set to continue, with the clock showing 80 minutes and Connacht leading by two points after Keith Matthews had scored the only try of the game. However, after Shaun Connor had missed with a drop goal attempt, Connacht dawdled over the restart on their 22 and referee Rob Dickson penalised them, much to their disbelief, allowing Connor a simple kick to win the game.

Speaking after the game, Lyn Jones acknowledged that the Ospreys were out of form, admitting he feared for his team when they went into European battle the following weekend: "We're right at the bottom of our game at the moment and we've got a lot of work to do... If we kick as badly and as openly against Stade Français next week they will cut us apart."

He might have been expecting the worst against Stade, beaten finalists the previous season, but the Ospreys produced a backs against the wall performance to be proud of at the Liberty, a ferocious defensive display in the second half ensuring a well-deserved and memorable win for the home team.

Sonny Parker set his team on the way to victory, taking advantage of a Shaun Connor dummy to cruise home under the posts for a 10–3 half-time lead. Stade dominated after the break, but were restricted to a single try in the corner from Lucas Borges as the Ospreys held on for a famous 13–8 win.

Barry Williams was a proud but relieved captain at the whistle: "We've let ourselves down all season but

Try scorer Steve Tandy competes for the ball against Gloucester, ably supported by Jason Spice and Lyndon Bateman

Adrian Cashmore shrugs off three Leicester players to put the Ospreys in front at half-time at Welford Road

we set a benchmark today that we can't step below again. The defence was awesome, the boys did a great job, and we held on. Now we've got to go to Clermont Auvergne next week and probably put in an even better performance to win out there."

Unfortunately, they were unable to reach the same level of performance two weeks running as they were outclassed in France, going down 34–14 despite a Shane Williams try in the fourth minute giving the Ospreys a dream start.

With nine players on international duty with Wales, a quiet November saw just one fixture, a 20–12 win at Ravenhill over Ulster, before December began with a classic contest in the Anglo-Welsh.

With both teams already eliminated from the competition, the Ospreys and Bristol cut loose at the Memorial Ground in a game of nine tries. It was the visitors who came out on top, 43–28, as recent signings Cashmore (2) and Karauna helped themselves to tries, with further Ospreys touchdowns coming from Steve Tandy and James Bater.

Spirits buoyed by some good recent form, the Ospreys headed to Welford Road to tackle Leicester Tigers in the first leg of the two-game European double-header. They welcomed back Gavin Henson for his first appearance since the Lions tour, having undergone groin surgery in the summer, and he was heavily involved as his team had the better of the early exchanges.

Indeed, it was his inside pass that released Parker for the opening try, and after Cashmore had gone over in first-half injury time, the Ospreys led 12–6.

However, Leicester hit back in some style in the second half, four tries and 24 points going unanswered as they claimed what was, in the end, a resounding 30–12 win.

With a return game at the Liberty just seven days later, there was a feeling in the Ospreys camp that they were hard done by at Welford Road, with both Henson and his coach Lyn Jones voicing their concerns about Tigers tactics and the lack of support from the officials.

The stage was set for a cracker, and the rematch certainly didn't disappoint. With a crowd of more than 13,000 creating a wonderful atmosphere at the Liberty, the Ospreys' forward dominance saw them take control early on as tries from Barry Williams and Shaun Connor looked likely to send them on their way to victory.

With Leicester down to 13 after yellow cards for Ollie Smith and Louis Deacon, the Ospreys then camped on the Leicester line with a series of scrums – Martin Corry fortunate not to become the third player sent to the bin – and with the visitors creaking there only seemed one outcome, but somehow they survived and were able to clear their lines.

Leicester rallied, a try from Leon Lloyd keeping them in touch as the game moved into the final quarter and, although Henson then missed an easy penalty, the Ospreys still seemed safe. However, with time up, the visitors launched one last, desperate attack as Tom Varndell carried out from his own 22, sparking a length of the field break that culminated in Dan Hipkiss going over. Andy Goode converted with the last kick of the game to break Ospreys' hearts and secure an unlikely 17–15 win.

There was a touchline row between the two benches at the final whistle, while the fallout from the game saw

Lyn Jones watches on in disbelief as the Ospreys fall to defeat at the hands of Leicester at the Liberty

lengthy bans for Henson and his team-mate Ian Evans after off-the-ball clashes with Alejandro Moreno and Harry Ellis respectively. What was to become one of 21st century rugby's great rivalries was born.

There was no time for the Ospreys to wallow in self-pity after being eliminated from the Heineken Cup with two games still to play, as there was just a four-day turnaround until the festive derby matches got underway.

Injuries in the second and back rows were mounting up, with the likes of Brent Cockbain, Ryan Jones and Andy Lloyd all nursing long-term injuries, so Des Dillon was brought in on a short-term loan from Leinster to provide some much needed cover.

It wasn't to be a happy Christmas for the region, who tasted defeat twice, against Cardiff Blues at the Liberty and away to the Dragons, with a trip to Stradey Park to face the Scarlets postponed because of a frozen pitch. After the Dragons defeat, Lyn Jones admitted he was disappointed with his team's performance, suggesting that "maybe the party from winning the Celtic League last year is finally over".

With that harsh reality staring them in the face, the Ospreys returned to European action when they welcomed Clermont Auvergne to the Liberty in mid January. There was just pride at stake for both teams, but it was the Ospreys who came out on top, Richard Mustoe and Stefan Terblanche scoring tries as Adrian Cashmore kicked 16 points to help his team to a 26–12 win.

The Heineken Cup came to a disappointing conclusion in Paris a week later as Stade Français ran in seven tries to inflict a 43–10 defeat on the Ospreys as they attempted in vain to secure their own passage into the last eight.

The season had begun so positively but, alas, the Ospreys were out of contention on all three fronts by the end of January. It had proven a disappointing start to life at the Liberty Stadium, but the Ospreys needed to pick themselves up and get straight back to business in the Celtic League to ensure European qualification for the following season.

That task wasn't being helped by an ever-growing injury list, with Barry Williams and Paul James forced

Richard Mustoe's try helps the Ospreys to a win over Clermont Auvergne

to undergo surgery, but the Ospreys showed good spirit in winning comfortably in Glasgow, Adrian Cashmore scoring their only try in a 22–8 win.

That was followed by a 22–18 victory against Borders at the Liberty, Andrew Bishop scoring the only try as Lyn Jones declared: "It hasn't been a good season but we'll keep plugging away."

However, next time out, the Ospreys were on the wrong end of a derby day thumping as Cardiff Blues secured a first ever double over the region, winning 40–14 at the Arms Park.

Despite the disappointing form on the field, it appeared that the Ospreys were making another step towards becoming a major player on the European scene off it, with the appointment of former Wales captain Paul Thorburn, now a highly respected commercial expert, as Strategic Development Manager.

According to Thorburn, his role would see him

"enhancing commercial and merchandising activity, targeting the business community, initiating community programmes and engaging all the feeder clubs within the region to make them feel a part of our success".

It remained a tough slog on the pitch though, the Ospreys' up and down form in the closing weeks being a mirror of the entire season.

They made heavy work of seeing off Edinburgh at the Liberty, winning 24–17 after being 21 points clear on 50 minutes, before going down to a 30–17 defeat in the rearranged derby against the Scarlets at Stradey Park at the end of March.

There was a narrow 16–13 win over Glasgow at the Liberty a week later, the Ospreys having to come from behind late on after tries from Richard Mustoe and Steve Tandy, Gavin Henson's 78th minute penalty winning it.

That was followed by the return game against the Scarlets, their local rivals' first ever visit to the Liberty, and they went home empty handed after a 25–13 Ospreys win in front of a 15,183 crowd. Gavin Henson scored 20 points with his boot, the extra five coming from a penalty try awarded at the scrum.

Leinster romped to a bonus-point win when they hosted the Ospreys on the final weekend of April, the 38–21 success putting them top of the table ahead of Irish rivals Ulster with just three games to go.

Back to back wins over Munster (27–10 at the Liberty) and Connacht (44–16 on the road) meant that the Ospreys had secured their Heineken Cup spot by the time that Ulster arrived in Swansea on the final day of the season knowing that a win would see them

pip Leinster to the title after the Dublin outfit's 40–31 defeat at Cardiff Blues.

The Ospreys were not simply going to lie down and surrender their Celtic League crown on their own patch though, regardless of how disappointing their season had been.

Ulster led 13–10 at the break, a Matt McCullough try and eight points from the boot of David Humphreys in response to Jonny Vaughton's early score and five from Henson's boot.

Humphreys then extended Ulster's lead early in the second half, only for a Jason Spice try, converted by Henson, to threaten to spoil the party and hand the title to Leinster. However, up stepped Humphreys again, with 78 minutes gone, to slot over a long-range penalty, via both uprights, to secure the win, and the Celtic League title.

The scene of the Ulster players celebrating a first ever title on the Liberty turf in front of their traveling fans would have been a galling one for the Ospreys. The message to them, ahead of 2006/07, was to use that pain to inspire them to bigger and better things next season.

4

The **2005/06 season could** very much be considered a coming of age campaign for the Ospreys off the field, with the move to the Liberty Stadium proving a catalyst for growth in the business that could never have been anticipated at the inception of regional rugby in 2003.

Average crowds had doubled and sales of the replica jersey had soared, with in excess of 38,000 snapped up by rugby fans keen to be associated with the growing brand of the Ospreys.

Incredibly, that made it the second biggest selling rugby club jersey in the UK and Ireland, a position it would hold unchallenged for the next seven years and counting. The shirt itself was also able to claim a UK record as the most valuable in British rugby as a sponsorship package worth more than half a million pounds was announced ahead of the new campaign.

The knock-on effect of this was that Ospreys became the first of the four Welsh regions to declare an operating profit, with the books showing a surplus of more than £300,000 in the accounts for the season just ended.

Of course, as the Ospreys' business grew so too did expectation on the field, and the weight of that expectation had proved too much in 2005/06 with a season that had kicked off promising so much ending up a huge anticlimax.

The directors at the Ospreys had spoken publicly about having "a five-year business plan in place that will help us achieve our premier target of being considered one of European rugby's elite clubs, both commercially and in terms of playing success."

A statement continued: "We want to be in a position where if ever a European league, or a Euro-12 type competition came into existence, the Ospreys would be one of the first names suggested as a member club."

With one Magners League title in the bank it was clear that more was expected, and the strong performance off the field enabled the board to invest strongly in the squad ahead of the second season at their new home, with the announcement of the signing of six international players.

Welsh internationals Lee Byrne and Tal Selley were confirmed from the Scarlets, while Scottish winger Nikki Walker arrived from Borders, but it was the signing of a trio of former All Blacks that really caught the eye and sent ripples throughout the world game.

Scrum-half Justin Marshall, with 81 appearances for New Zealand making him the most capped

New training facilities, but it's still a case of 'do it yourself' for the Ospreys

half-back in his country's history, was first to be announced. It was a signing described by Mike Cuddy as "massive" and he added that "to have secured a player of Justin's quality is testament to the progress we have made since our formation barely three years ago."

Marshall was joined in Ospreys colours by a big, experienced physical number eight called Filo Tiatia. A 35-year-old who had spent the last four years playing in Japan, he would go on to make a huge impression at the region. The third former All Black was another back row, 29-year-old Jonno Gibbes, captain of Waikato Chiefs and the NZ Maori team.

It wasn't all inward traffic, with the inevitable player departures to balance the squad. Among others, out went Andy Newman (Glasgow), James Bater (Scarlets) and Adrian Cashmore (retired), while

Damian Karauna took up a support role behind the scenes. However, the level of team strengthening meant that a repeat of the previous season's failure to secure silverware seemed unthinkable.

The man to lead the Ospreys into action in the new campaign was named as Duncan Jones, the experienced loose head taking over the captaincy permanently after deputising for the injured Barry Williams the previous season.

Duncan's namesake, Derwyn, also had new responsibilities for the new season following a sideways move from Team Manager duties to growing the organisation's relationship with its member clubs.

August saw news of a historic fixture scheduled for the Liberty that autumn, with confirmation that the Ospreys would become the first region to play a major touring nation when they entertained Australia on 1st November.

Although still more than two months away, the buzz surrounding the fixture was huge and it soon became apparent that the region were heading for yet another first – the first 20,520 capacity crowd at their new home.

Meanwhile, pre-season was rounded off with the team's only 'proper' warm-up game, a 24–14 win over Harlequins in a fiery encounter at the Liberty. Justin Marshall impressed on his first start for the region as James Hook, Lee Byrne and Jonny Vaughton touched down.

After a summer of eye-catching recruitment it was essential that the Ospreys got the season off to a winning start, and it was Edinburgh who were outgunned on the opening weekend of the newly-named Magners League, a Byrne try and four penalties from Hook securing a 17–11 home win.

There was a setback in the opening week of September when it transpired that supposed summer signing Jonno Gibbes wouldn't be joining the region after all, the Kiwi doing a U-turn on his original decision to sign for the Ospreys by recommitting to the Chiefs for the following year instead of heading to South Wales upon completion of the season in New Zealand.

Round two of the Magners League saw a disappointing defeat in Galway as Connacht overturned a seven-point half-time deficit, which came courtesy of Marshall's first Ospreys try, to record a 15–10 win at the Sportsground.

Crazy scheduling then saw the Ospreys playing two home games inside 72 hours, but a strong squad effort duly delivered back-to-back wins at the Liberty, a narrow 18–16 derby success against Cardiff Blues and a 30–13 victory over Borders.

They were brought crashing back down to earth a week later though when they were thumped 43–7 by Ulster at Ravenhill, their third game in just nine days. Second-half yellow cards for Ryan and Alun Wyn Jones proved costly after Gavin Henson had given them an early lead, as defending champions Ulster moved back to the top of the early season table.

With three wins and two defeats in their opening five league games, the Ospreys finally began to find some consistency when they switched competitions and went into the Anglo-Welsh tournament, now known as the EDF Energy Cup.

First up was a home tie against strongly fancied Gloucester, who were sent home with their tails between

New signing Justin Marshall takes control

their legs after a six-try, 49–16 defeat at the hands of the Ospreys – Barry Williams, Justin Marshall, Gavin Henson, Shane Williams and Sonny Parker (2) all touching down.

Ahead of the second fixture, away to Bath, came the announcement of a key off-field appointment, former Welsh international and Swansea RFC captain Kevin Hopkins as the first ever Director of Rugby at the region.

Hopkins assumed responsibility for the strategic development and management of the Ospreys squad, to create a sustained and evolving rugby plan within the region.

Back on the pitch, Bath were seen off 31–24 as the Ospreys edged towards their first ever Anglo-Welsh semi-final, before a third straight win came at the Liberty as Glasgow were defeated 26–9 in the Magners League.

The opening fixture of the Ospreys' Heineken Cup campaign saw reigning English champions Sale heading to the Liberty Stadium, on a night that was to become the first of the region's truly great occasions at the state-of-the-art venue.

On a night of high drama in front of almost 14,000 fans, the Ospreys scored the latest of late tries to secure an incredible 17–16 victory. It was ten-all at the break, Shane Williams and Juan Fernández Lobbe scoring a try apiece, only for two second-half Charlie Hodgson penalties to seemingly win it for the English side.

However, the Ospreys were able to pick themselves up off the canvas for one last rally and, after multiple phases, they were able to fashion a try in the corner for Williams, his second of the match, cutting the lead to a solitary point with the clock showing that it came in the eighth additional minute.

There was still work to do, but James Hook made a difficult kick on the right-hand touchline look easy, sparking wild celebrations in the stands and on the pitch.

As is the nature of Europe's elite competition though, there was no time to dwell on such a memorable victory as the sizable challenge of French aristocrats Stade Français in Paris lie ahead.

It was a daunting task, one that had proven beyond 24 of the 25 teams to have previously undertaken it in the Heineken Cup – including the Ospreys themselves who had endured a 43–10 hammering the previous season.

It was a definite improvement this time around but, ultimately, a failure to take their chances proved costly. The Ospreys started brightly, Sonny Parker scoring an excellent early try, but Gavin Henson missed four kicks allowing Stade to go in 9–7 to the good at the break. The visitors kept in the hunt in the second half, thanks to a Lee Byrne try, but they faded badly in the final quarter as the French finally put daylight between the teams, winning 27–14.

Stade coach, Fabien Galthié, was a relieved man after the match, declaring: "The Ospreys are an excellent team. The kicking was the difference between the two sides."

From the Ospreys dressing room, Justin Marshall echoed those thoughts, saying: "It hurts that we failed to capitalise on our opportunities. We had the chances to put them away but we made too many errors at crucial points in the game."

Shane Williams races through to score a dramatic late try against Sale in the first Heineken Cup tie of the new season…

...and James Hook converts to win it against the English champions

Shaun Connor keeps the Ospreys in touch with Australia

There would be a chance to put things right later in the season, but for now the focus was about the historic clash against the touring Wallabies just four days later.

A sell-out crowd was confirmed, and the build-up to the game had seen a real buzz around the region on such a special occasion, with every single one of the 72 clubs within the region to be represented at the Liberty Stadium on the night.

The concept of regional rugby had really struggled to catch the imagination of the wider rugby public across Wales in the three years since its inception, but this was a fixture that had really fired appetites for the product within the Ospreys' boundaries.

The commonly held view was that the Ospreys were the only 'true' region in Wales, a viewpoint that was cemented two days before the international clash when Ordnance Survey, Britain's national mapping agency, formally recognised the geographical region of 'Ospreylia'.

Embracing the whole of Swansea, Neath Port Talbot and Bridgend, as well as the southern tip of Powys, Ordnance Survey measured Ospreylia at 37 miles east to west and 24 miles from its northern most point to the coastline of the south, with a total boundary measuring 151 miles.

So, it was Ospreylia v Australia at the Liberty Stadium, and although at times the quality of the rugby on display left more than a little to be desired, the contest was full of passion and commitment from both sides.

There was little to separate the teams for 70 minutes, Adam Ashley-Cooper scoring the opening try for Australia before Barry Williams responded for the Ospreys. The Wallabies' Cameron Shepherd traded penalties with Shaun Connor to leave it all square at 13–13 at half-time.

After a point-less third quarter, Shepherd then nudged the tourists ahead before Connor's third penalty levelled it again on 70 minutes. The ever-reliable number ten then slotted a drop goal to put the Ospreys in front for the first time with just seven minutes to go.

As Australia frantically launched an attack from inside their own half, looking to steal the game at the death, Richard Mustoe showed great awareness to intercept Mark Gerard's pass and gallop home from 40 metres out to seal a famous win for Ospreylia.

Speaking post-match, Lyn Jones spoke of his pride at what his team had achieved:

I'm very proud of the players and I'm pleased for everybody in the region. This is a massive result for rugby in South Wales. We only have a short history but we've already been through some ups and downs and taken plenty of kickings, but look around this place tonight and you see more than 20,000 people here to watch us beating Australia. To me, that says we are heading in the right direction in Ospreylia, whatever the critics have to say about regional rugby.

A 25–20 defeat away to Munster in their first competition fixture post-Wallabies clash served as a stark reminder that they needed to stay focused and they responded positively, winning five of their six matches in December.

First up was a 34–3 home win over Bristol to secure a first ever Anglo-Welsh Cup semi-final spot, with the draw throwing up a Welsh derby against Cardiff Blues at the Millennium Stadium in March. In the Heineken Cup, back-to-back wins over Italians Calvisano kept the Ospreys hopes alive after the setback against Stade Français.

There were three Welsh derbies in the space of eight Christmas days, the first of which saw the Blues win 30–24 at the Arms Park.

A season of historic and memorable occasions continued on Boxing Day when a second capacity crowd of the campaign welcomed local rivals, the Scarlets, to the Liberty. Those present were treated to another spectacular win for the Ospreys who scored five tries on their way to a crushing 50–24 win.

As 2006 drew to a close, the Dragons were seen off

Richard Mustoe races through to score a historic try

The Ospreys celebrate a memorable win over the touring Wallabies

12–6 in monsoon conditions at the Liberty, before the first game of the new year saw a much changed and unfamiliar line-up put to the sword by Leinster, the Irish province winning 45–22 in Dublin.

Stade Français were next, visiting the Liberty Stadium for the Heineken Cup return clash the following weekend. Not for the first time that season, the Liberty was the venue for 80 minutes of high drama of the highest quality.

The hosts had started slowly, allowing Stade to build up a 13-point lead early in the second half. The boot of James Hook helped the Ospreys to chip away at the deficit with two penalties, before Nikki Walker finished off a flowing move to score under the posts. Hook's conversion levelled things with eleven minutes to go and then his penalty in the 76th minute, the first time the Ospreys had led, looked to have won it.

However, with the clock showing time, Ospreys hands were spotted in the ruck and Lionel Beauxis made no mistake with a monster 50m effort from wide on the right to break Ospreys' hearts, his kick levelling things at 22-each.

Post-match, Ryan Jones held his hand up to acknowledge he was the guilty party penalised. "It was me who gave away the penalty" he said. "I didn't think he would make it from that range, but he did, and I had to say sorry in the dressing room afterwards."

Ahead of the final pool three match in Sale, Derwyn Jones, who had undertaken a new role within the regional set-up three months earlier, announced that he was leaving the Ospreys to seek a new challenge.

To have any hope of securing a Heineken quarter-final place, the Ospreys needed to defeat Sale and then hope for results elsewhere to go their way, leaving them in the hunt for one of the two best runners-up spots. The team did their bit, Steve Tandy and Stefan Terblanche scoring a try each in an 18–7 win.

The lack of a try bonus point after a dominant performance proved costly though; Leicester's incredible win in Munster (a first ever Thomond Park defeat in the competition for Munster) and Northampton's losing bonus point at home to Biarritz ensuring that Ospreys interests were ended for another year.

Nevertheless, the Ospreys remained well placed to contest silverware on the two remaining fronts and three straight wins during the Six Nations period over Ulster (29–22), Connacht (31–10) and Edinburgh (30–12) kept their Magners League hopes alive.

With their international contingent back in the fold following a disappointing Six Nations, it was destination Millennium Stadium next, and a derby clash against the Blues in the EDF Energy Cup, with a first ever visit to Twickenham awaiting the winners.

A masterclass of scrum-half rugby from Justin Marshall had the Ospreys on the front foot from very early on and their dominance was rewarded with a 27–10 victory to secure that place in the final. Tries came from Sonny Parker and Lee Byrne, with James Hook kicking 17 points as the Ospreys looked ahead to their big day out at HQ, where Leicester would provide the opposition in three weeks' time.

Prior to that date, there was the small matter of a home game against Munster in the Magners, Hook and Marshall getting all the points between them in a 20–12 success.

A two-mile convoy of coaches departed the Liberty Stadium for Twickenham on Sunday, 15th April as 10,000 fans travelled in hope that the Ospreys could record their first win over the Tigers, at the home of English rugby. As Roger Blyth said ahead of the match: "It has been a memorable season for us so far and Sunday's game is the first in a run of fixtures that could see us turn the 2006/07 campaign from a memorable one to a magnificent one."

On a baking hot afternoon in south-west London, the Ospreys suffered a nightmare first 40, conceding four tries in an error-strewn opening as Leicester raced into a 28–9 half-time lead, three James Hook penalties all they had to show for their efforts.

A much improved second half showing saw the Ospreys give their fans fresh hope, a Shane Williams double and a try from Lee Byrne bringing them back to within touching distance.

Sonny Parker celebrates one of his two tries against Borders that helped clinch a second title for the Ospreys

However, a fifth Leicester try, followed by a penalty, put daylight between the two teams once again, and although Nikki Walker dotted down for the Ospreys fourth try with five minutes to go, ultimately they'd given themselves too much to do. Leicester claimed the silverware with a 41–35 success, double try scorer Shane Williams summing things up when he said afterwards: "You just can't give a team like Leicester the start we did."

Despite the disappointment at defeat in the final, the Ospreys could hold their heads up high after matching one of England's leading teams blow for blow in a major Cup final, their approach to the game and second-half spirit winning many plaudits.

Coaches Sean Holley and Lyn Jones hold the Magners League trophy aloft as James Hook joins in the celebrations

Joint Managing Directors, Roger Blyth (L) and Mike Cuddy celebrate Magners League success

There was still one more chance for silverware though, and an opportunity to regain the Magners League crown they'd won two years previous. Due to their EDF run it was going to have to be done the hard way, though. With two rearranged games to be scheduled in, it meant that the Ospreys had to play catch-up and faced five games in 18 days, four of them on the road.

First up was the short nine-mile trip across the Loughor estuary to face closest rivals the Scarlets. It was the perfect start to the end-of-season run-in, James Hook steering his team to a 19–6 win as he scored all the points, including rounding off a trademark Shane Williams length-of-the-field run to score the game's only try.

Three days later it was back to the Liberty for the final home game of the campaign against Leinster.

The Ospreys went into the game in third place, a point behind second placed Ulster and trailing their opponents, who led the table, by four. If the Magners League trophy was coming back to the Liberty Stadium, an Ospreys win was essential.

As expected, it was an edgy, nip and tuck game with little to separate the two sides. It was all square at the break, a Justin Marshall try and five points from Shaun Connor's boot seemingly enough to give the hosts a seven-point half-time lead only for Shane Horgan's try, converted by Felipe Contepomi, to level it at the break, 10–10.

Contepomi then converted his own try early in the second half to give another five-figure crowd the jitters, but James Hook, on for Connor, kicked the team to victory with three penalties.

The 19–17 win meant that the Ospreys had gone the

Inside the dressing room as the Ospreys celebrate

entire season unbeaten at home, in all competitions and friendlies, and with a 100 per cent record at the Liberty in the Magners League.

It also moved the Ospreys up into second place, two points behind Leinster and one ahead of third placed Cardiff Blues after Ulster fell to fourth place. While Leinster had just two games remaining, the Ospreys and the Blues both had an extra game. It was going down to the wire.

Cardiff Blues played their game in hand four days later, a 31–20 win over the Dragons seeing them leapfrogging both the Ospreys and Leinster to go top.

The first of the three remaining games ended disappointingly as the Ospreys could only muster a losing bonus point in a 29–26 defeat to Glasgow. A dazzling start with three tries in the first 26 minutes proved in vain as they failed to add a point in the second half, Dan Parks kicking the Scots to victory.

With the Blues losing to the Scarlets and Leinster defeating Borders that weekend, it meant that the Dublin-based team were now six points clear of the Ospreys in third place with the Blues sandwiched in between.

The final week of the campaign saw the Ospreys playing twice – knowing that even two wins could possibly not be enough to secure the title.

First up was the short trip to the Dragons, the game in hand on both teams above them. The Ospreys made light work of the Gwent side as they secured a bonus-point win, 27–13, with tries from Andy Lloyd, Filo Tiatia and Shane Williams (2), to move back into second spot, a point behind Leinster and two ahead of the Blues.

That result meant it was all down to the final weekend, which saw third-placed Blues entertain leaders Leinster on the Friday night, while the Ospreys travelled north to face Borders 24 hours later, a game that was to be the Scottish side's last ever following the decision of their Union to disband them.

A Leinster bonus-point win at the Arms Park would have secured them the title, but it never looked likely as Cardiff took the five points themselves to jump to the top of the table. That meant the Ospreys simply needed a win at Netherdale the following evening, bonus point or not, to be crowned as champions. Any other outcome would see the title go to the Blues.

On an emotional evening, a nervy Ospreys just about did enough to secure a second title in three years, holding off a late Borders rally to win 24–16. An early Filo Tiatia try was followed by two from Sonny Parker to put the Ospreys well in control before ten quick points from the Scots cut the lead to just five with under ten minutes to go. It took a long-range penalty from James Hook to settle the nerves and secure the title.

After a long season of ups and downs, the Ospreys had managed to secure silverware ensuring they hadn't ended the season empty-handed. A first major Cup final appearance and a best ever performance in Europe, where they were unfortunate not to progress out of the pool stage for the first time, along with a league title, had cemented the region's position as the leading team in Wales after just four years of existence.

The question everybody wanted answered was just how far could the Ospreys fly?

5

Transfer activity at the Liberty Stadium during the close season made it abundantly clear that expectations at the Ospreys were continuing to grow.

New arrivals included experienced Welsh internationals in the shape of former Swansea centre Mark Taylor, a Grand Slam winner and British and Irish Lion, who signed from Sale where he had won a Premiership title, along with the evergreen second row Ian Gough, signed from the Dragons.

Also arriving at the Ospreys was Cardiff Blues scrum-half Mike Phillips, another highly rated Wales cap, with Jason Spice moving in the opposite direction, signing for the Blues after three years at the Liberty in what amounted to a straight swap.

Just weeks before the season got underway it was announced that All Black legend Marty Holah, regarded as one of the finest openside flankers in world rugby, had signed and would join the region at the end of October upon completion of the season in New Zealand.

With the Rugby World Cup set to get underway in France, the Ospreys entered pre-season minus twelve players who were involved in the competition, but the absentees seemed to make no difference as the action got underway.

There was a relatively trouble free afternoon in Berkshire as they saw off the challenge of Newbury 43–15, running in seven tries with youngsters Gareth Owen and Dan Biggar catching the eye. That was followed by a 27–15 win over Bristol at the Liberty, and the Ospreys were seemingly set fair for the new campaign.

Their Magners League defence got underway at the end of August, the Welsh regions having to start early ahead of the Rugby World Cup to enable them to fit the extra games involved in the Anglo-Welsh competition, meaning the campaign started with back-to-back Welsh derbies before the summer was out.

First up was a trip to Cardiff Arms Park where the Blues had an early opportunity for revenge on the Ospreys who had pipped them to the title just three months earlier. It was the hosts who came out on top in a game dominated by the boot after Shaun Connor missed a penalty attempt to win the game in the dying seconds, leaving the final score 17–15 to the home team.

The Ospreys had gone the entire previous season unbeaten at the Liberty Stadium, with a 100 per cent home record in the league, but they meekly surrendered that run eleven days later when the Scarlets headed back west across the Loughor Bridge with the points having won a scrappy contest 14–9.

This wasn't the start that the defending champions wanted, missing a dozen at the Rugby World Cup or

Marty Holah made an instant impact on his arrival in Ospreylia from New Zealand

not, but it got even worse after another narrow defeat, this time at Ravenhill against Ulster. The Ospreys were trailing 14–3 just short of the hour before a Connor charge-down led to Andrew Bishop scoring the team's first try of the new season and, in a nail-biting finish, Connor was able to add a couple of penalties to take the Ospreys two points ahead with three minutes left on the clock.

Ulster responded with a Niall O'Connor kick in the 79th minute to edge back in front to win it, 17–16.

The eagerly awaited first win of the season finally came at the fourth attempt when Glasgow were thumped 37–23 at the Liberty Stadium, Lee Byrne scoring two tries and young flanker Ben Lewis also touching down. It was a special occasion for hooker Barry Williams, who became the first Osprey to reach 100 appearances for the region, a landmark hailed by Lyn Jones, who said: "Barry is an inspirational leader, he is an Osprey through and through and he deserves everything the game can offer him, including being the first Osprey to reach the milestone of 100 competitive appearances."

While Williams was aiming to build on his 100 appearances, one player coming to the end of his Ospreys career was South African Stefan Terblanche. Having returned home to play for the Sharks on loan the previous summer, the former Springbok had reached agreement with Ospreys management to be released from his contract a year early to return to Durban and sign a permanent deal with the Sharks.

His 87th and final Ospreys appearance would be

Richard Hibbard scores to round off a great Heineken Cup win over Gloucester in the Liberty Stadium rain

against Edinburgh on the first weekend of October, bringing to an end four years at the region. Speaking about his time at the Ospreys, Terblanche said: "When I joined the region the Ospreys were just a name, a vision, and a group of players. The organisation has now grown into one of the most professional outfits in world rugby with two Magners League titles, an EDF Energy Cup final and beating the Aussies being the obvious highlights during my time."

He was unable to sign off with a win as it finished 13-apiece in Edinburgh, as once again a late missed penalty cost the Ospreys a win, this time Gareth Owen missing the target.

Wales' disappointingly early exit from the Rugby World Cup following defeat to Fiji in their final pool game meant that the Ospreys were boosted by the early return of the international contingent, with ten of their eleven Wales squad members plus Scotland's Nikki Walker all selected to feature in the home game against Munster, the final Magners game for a month.

They had a positive impact on Ospreys fortunes as well, inspiring the team to only a second win of the season, 16–3.

A new face arrived at the region in the week of the Munster win as Tongan international back row Hale T-Pole, who had made a huge impact at the World Cup in France, signed until the end of the season.

Having reached the final of the previous year's EDF Energy Cup, where they lost a thriller to Leicester Tigers, the Ospreys were determined to go one better this time around.

They got off to a flying start in the first round of fixtures in the 2007/08 competition with an emphatic victory on the road against Worcester at their Sixways

Ryan Jones celebrates the Ospreys' first ever win in France, defeating Bourgoin to clinch a place in the Heineken Cup last eight for the first time

ground. Shane Williams and Lee Byrne both touched down twice while Sonny Parker, Mike Phillips and Nikki Walker also crossed the line in a 47–16 win.

If that result hadn't made people sit up and take notice, then what came the following week certainly did. The Ospreys, with Marty Holah making his debut off the bench, were rampant as they tore London Irish to shreds at the Liberty Stadium. Shane Williams grabbed a hat-trick as the Ospreys once again ran in seven tries, the others coming from Jonathan Thomas, Ben Lewis, Alun Wyn Jones and Mike Phillips as it finished 51–16.

With the Heineken Cup up next, and a home game against French side Bourgoin, Lyn Jones was quick to keep his players' feet on the ground as they once again went into European battle hoping to progress past the group stage for the first time. Jones said: "London Irish gave us the challenge we hoped for in the first half but in the second there was only one side in it. We expect a completely different challenge from Bourgoin next week… We scored 40 points last week, 50 this week, but next Saturday there could be one score in it."

Jones' warning was spot on, as the winning margin for the Ospreys as they kicked-off their European campaign was exactly the one score, Gavin Henson scoring the only try and James Hook kicking 17 points in a 22–15 win at the Liberty.

It was a case of the 'chances that got away' a week later as Gloucester somehow claimed a 26–18 win over the Ospreys at Kingsholm to take control of pool two, despite an, at times, dominant performance from the visitors. Two first-half tries from Sonny Parker put them in the driving seat, but after Jonny Vaughton somehow contrived to make a hash of a clear run-in and James Hook was off target with some kickable penalties, Gloucester fought back strongly to deny the Ospreys even a losing bonus point.

The mishmash of a season structure meant that it was back to the Magners for one week, before the final EDF pool match and two more Heineken Cup games, and with Wales also squeezing in an extra post-World Cup match against champions South Africa, it meant that the Ospreys faced a full strength Leinster at the Liberty minus nine internationals plus another seven injured players.

It was no surprise therefore that Leinster won, 26–15, but there was one bright spot for the Ospreys with a debut off the bench for 17-year-old Ashley Beck from Skewen, who became the youngest ever player to feature in a Magners League game.

The following weekend saw the Ospreys face Harlequins at the Twickenham Stoop, with the winner securing an EDF Energy Cup semi-final spot. In truth, it was a poor game, but nevertheless proved a memorable contest in many ways.

At one stage in the first half the Ospreys had been reduced to twelve men with Paul James, Lee Byrne and Gavin Henson all in the sin-bin, but a combination of poor attacking play and resilient defence saw the Ospreys go in at the break 6–3 ahead, thanks to two Henson penalties. It was the Henson story again after the break, as he kept the Ospreys in front with two more penalties before sealing the win at the death with an interception try which he converted to round off a 19–8 success.

With one cup knock-out spot secured, the Ospreys then faced Magners League rivals Ulster in a Heineken double-header and they kept up the pressure on Gloucester with two impressive victories, a seven try 48–17 romp at the Liberty followed by a 16–8 win in Belfast.

In between the two wins came the announcement that two players were leaving the Ospreys, with Richie Pugh released to represent Wales on the IRB Sevens circuit while big second row Brent Cockbain was joining Sale Sharks.

As the Ospreys prepared for the Christmas derby fixtures, the big news from the region was the appointment of New Zealander Andrew Hore as the first ever Elite Performance Director at the region.

The appointment of Hore, who had recently rejected the opportunity to take up the same post at the WRU, was seen in the game as a significant coup for the Ospreys. Familiar to rugby people in Wales having spent four years working with the WRU earlier in the decade, Hore was leaving his role as High Performance Manager with the NZRU and would arrive in Ospreylia in the New Year.

He would initially oversee a review of the entire organisation before reporting his findings back to the board, which would then form the basis of a business plan to allow the Ospreys to "fully reach their potential at the top of the European game".

It's the Little & Large show as Ian Evans congratulates Shane Williams on one of his brace of tries in the EDF Energy Cup semi-final versus Saracens

First up was Gloucester at the Liberty Stadium, and sensing the importance of the clash, a crowd in excess of 18,000 packed in on a horrendous, wet January evening. It was a must-win game if the Ospreys were to keep alive their hopes of progressing, but the result was never in doubt as they produced one of their all-time best performances to brush aside the current English Premiership leaders.

A Shane Williams try and 14 points from James Hook ensured a half-time lead of 19–3, and although Gloucester rallied after the break, majestic performances from New Zealanders Justin Marshall and Filo Tiatia ensured that the Ospreys didn't buckle as they had in the first game, a late Richard Hibbard try and eight more from Hook's boot ensuring a 32–15 win.

The result meant that all the Ospreys needed to do now to book a place in the last eight was win in France the following weekend – something they had never before managed!

The Ospreys travelled to Stade Pierre Rajon in South-Eastern France in good spirits and, after a nervous start, they slowly took control of the contest with tries from Shane Williams and Lee Byrne in the second quarter giving them a twelve-point half-time lead that they wouldn't relinquish.

A Jonathan Thomas try on 79 minutes meant a late flurry of Bourgoin points in the final 90 seconds were meaningless, the 28–21 win securing the Ospreys passage into the last eight for the first time ever.

Christmas was very much a mixed bag, the Scarlets edging it 17–12 at Stradey Park before the Ospreys defeated Cardiff 22–3 at the Liberty in front of almost 17,000 people on New Year's Eve.

The beginning of 2008 began saw a 26–15 defeat in Leinster, but the real focus was the two remaining Heineken Cup pool two fixtures, with the region still very much in the hunt for a first ever quarter-final spot.

Tempers fray at Vicarage Road as Saracens go looking for revenge in the Heineken Cup quarter-final

Their status as one of the best runners-up meant they were handed an away tie, and they were drawn to travel to Vicarage Road in Watford to play first seeds Saracens – the same opposition they had been paired with in the last four of the EDF, meaning the two sides would go head-to-head in knockout rugby twice in as many weeks that spring.

In stark contrast to their impressive Cup form that had seen them lose just once in nine games, their Magners League title defence was as good as over already with just three wins in ten games so far. The position hardly improved in February though, as a comfortable 37–7 win over Connacht was followed by a 9–6 loss in the wind and rain of Glasgow.

It was little surprise that the league form was suffering though, given the interruptions of international rugby throughout the season, circumstances which, although the same for everybody, seemed to hit the Ospreys more than their rivals.

This was certainly the case at the start of the Six Nations when new Wales Head Coach, Warren Gatland, named an incredible 13 Ospreys in the starting XV for his first ever match, against England, with one more on the bench. It was an amazing achievement for the region, setting a new Welsh record for representation from one team in a Welsh starting line-up, but one that inevitably caused selection headaches for Lyn Jones and his coaching team.

As the Six Nations kicked on, the Magners League took a break once more, allowing supporters to enjoy a

second Grand Slam success in four seasons for Wales, again inspired by the Ospreys contingent.

At the Liberty Stadium, Andrew Hore finally arrived to take up his post during March, immediately starting work on his detailed review of operations at the region.

Returning to regional duty a week after their Grand

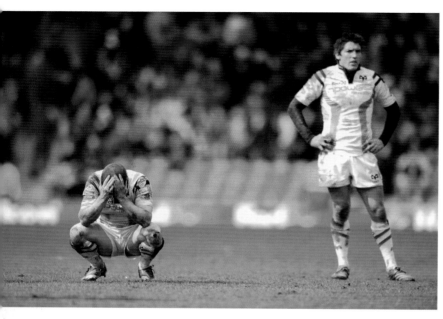

The anguish is clear as Shane Williams and James Hook contemplate an unexpected defeat at the hands of Saracens

display saw the Ospreys run away with it, finishing up 30–3 winners as Shane Williams (2), Gavin Henson, and Filo Tiatia all scored tries to secure a Twickenham rematch against last years conquerors, Leicester.

They maintained that form the following week to register a 32–7 bonus-point win over Ulster at the Liberty Stadium, before switching their focus back to Saracens in the second part of their knockout double bill.

After their performance and result just two weeks' earlier, the Ospreys were red-hot favourites going into the game, despite being the away team. However, fired up by skipper Ryan Jones' comments post-match in Cardiff that such was the Ospreys' dominance Saracens wouldn't have scored if they'd played till next week, the hosts flew into their opponents from the first whistle.

With England veteran Richard Hill to the fore, the home team never allowed the Ospreys to settle, forcing errors across the field, and in the end it finished 19–10 to Saracens, a deserved win against an Ospreys team that had failed to turn up.

Post-match Jones, appointed captain at the start of the season, acknowledged the job Saracens had done on his side, saying: "They did their homework on us and we came off second best in facets of the game. We failed to generate any sort of momentum and I think we were all affected by the pressure."

His thoughts were echoed by Lyn Jones who admitted he may have got the tactics wrong: "There are 100 ways of playing rugby and perhaps the one we selected today wasn't good enough. We didn't play very well."

Slam winning victory over France at the Millennium Stadium, the Ospreys' international contingent were on familiar ground as they returned to the same venue for the first of their two clashes with Saracens, in the EDF Energy Cup.

Throughout the Ospreys' history, coaches have wrestled with the issue of reintegrating their international contingent back into the squad, but there were no such problems on this occasions as they hit the ground running in front of 40,000 people at the home of Welsh rugby.

Leading 8–0 at half-time, a storming second-half

Ospreys fans flock to Twickenham for a revenge mission against Leicester, last year's EDF Energy Cup conquerors

Andrew Bishop scores at Twickenham

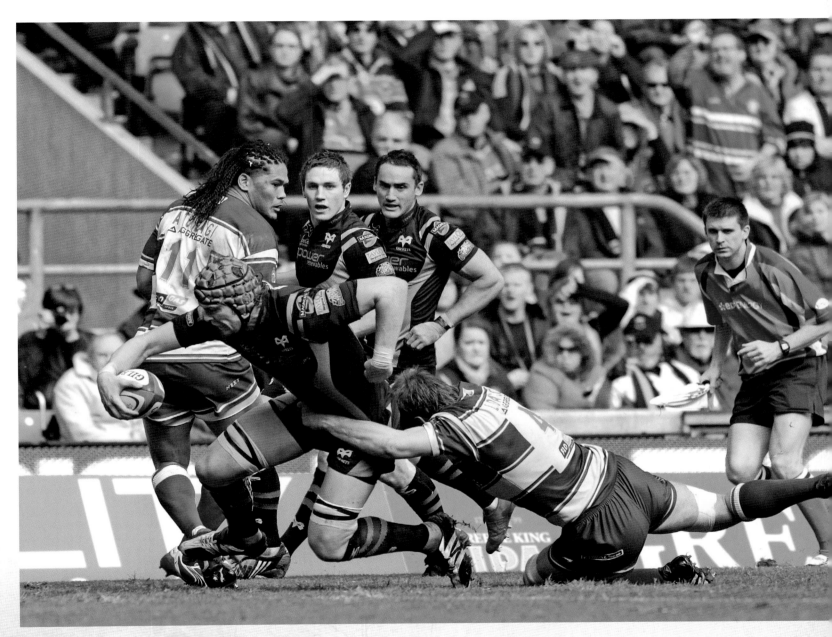

Alun Wyn Jones reaches for the Tigers tryline

Relief and celebrations as the Ospreys claim silverware once again

The games were coming thick and fast, and with a big Cup final against Leicester just a week away, there was a chance of immediate redemption for the Ospreys, not to mention revenge for the 41–35 defeat inflicted on them at the same venue the previous year.

This time, more than 15,000 fans made the exodus to South-West London to support the region, and they witnessed a performance that would restore pride in the Ospreys jersey.

The contest turned out to be a far cry from the carnival of running rugby that was the 2007 final, but that wouldn't have bothered anyone in the Ospreys camp as they dominated from first whistle to last, tries from Andrew Bishop and Alun Wyn Jones along with 13 points from James Hook securing the silverware as it finished 23–6.

It was an achievement to be proud of, and the players certainly celebrated in style as Ryan Jones collected the Cup, but there was an evident sense of relief in some of the post-match comments.

Man of the match Marty Holah admitted that it had been "tough to pick ourselves up after the loss to Saracens but we refocused in midweek," while the captain said he was "proud to have turned it around. It was just reward for the fantastic hard work we've put in this week."

In the build-up to the game the Ospreys' apparent inability to win the big one-off games had come under close media scrutiny, a viewpoint that the Saracens defeat had only given weight to. Reflecting that coverage Lyn Jones spoke passionately after the win, his delight evident to all.

> That was a very important turning point for us, we've crossed that line of getting a win in a big game…
> The Saracens defeat was a kick in the pants, we were devastated but there was a very positive attitude from everyone today. We're absolutely delighted, now we have to build on this success.

For one of the heroes of the win, Filo Tiatia, lifting the Cup was only the second most memorable event of the day. The crowd favourite had stayed behind in Swansea to be with his wife Sally as she gave birth to twin girls Gianna and Emina the night before the game. He then travelled to the team hotel in London in the early hours of matchday to catch just a few hours' rest

Filo Tiatia relaxes with twin girls Gianna and Emina, born on the morning of the Ospreys big Twickenham win

before playing a key role in the back row battle that helped win the game for the Ospreys.

With their hold on the Magners League long relinquished, the Ospreys faded badly post Twickenham, winning just one of their remaining five games as they slumped to a disappointing seventh place in the final table with just six victories all season – by far the worst performance in their ten-year history.

Nevertheless, there were still a few more notable landmarks before the season was out, with Shaun Connor becoming the second Ospreys centurion and youngster Kristian Phillips becoming both the youngest player to start a Magners League match and the youngest try scorer, in the last day of the season defeat to Connacht.

As the dust settled on a season of highs and lows – one that had seen the Ospreys secure silverware once again, yet suffer their worst Magners League showing; a campaign that had seen them progress to the knockout stages of the Heineken Cup for the first time, only to crash out in ignominious fashion – came the news that Lyn Jones, who had led the Ospreys as Head Coach since its inception, was to relinquish his post by 'mutual agreement'.

Speaking about the decision, Jones said:

We've come a very long way since the summer of 2003 when Neath and Swansea came together to form the Ospreys, and I take great satisfaction in our many achievements over the past five years... As someone born and bred in the area, this has been a very tough decision to make, but parting on a positive note after a successful season that saw the Ospreys become the first Welsh side to win the EDF Energy Cup is the best ending to a very enjoyable time.

Roger Blyth paid tribute to a man he described as:

... the most successful coach in Wales since the onset of regional rugby... He successfully led us through our challenging formative seasons, taking on probably one of the hardest jobs in UK rugby by successfully combining the rugby-playing cultures of Neath and Swansea into a new dynamic. He developed the squad into winners of the Celtic League in 2005 and 2007, and this season led the region into the European Cup quarter-finals as well as winning the EDF Energy Cup, while contributing 14 players to the Wales squad... The entire region owes Lyn a debt of gratitude for the work he has done for the Ospreys and our warmest wishes will go with him for whatever new coaching challenge he ultimately decides to undertake.

When Kevin Hopkins confirmed just days later that he too was leaving the Ospreys after turning down an alternative role within the organisation, it was clear that this was a time of change at the Liberty Stadium.

Backs Coach, Sean Holley, and Forwards Coach, Jonathan Humphreys, were to take joint charge of the team while the Ospreys searched for a replacement for Jones, someone who Blyth said would be:

... capable of picking up the reigns from Lyn to drive the region forward and accelerate our development. An individual of outstanding ability, professionalism, leadership and innovation with the capability of taking the squad on to the next level... This is a crucial appointment for the future of the Ospreys, and we need to make sure that we get it right in order to build on the success of the last five years. It is a decision that will take time and careful consideration, a process that will ensure we appoint the right man for the job.

Whoever that man was going to be, interesting times lay ahead for the Ospreys.

6

With Lyn Jones having departed, the new season marked the start of a new era for the Ospreys, albeit a new era without a leader, as yet.

The search for Jones' replacement continued as the players returned for pre-season, minus 19 senior and age-grade international representatives, which meant that coaching duo Sean Holley and Jonathan Humphreys took charge of the team in a joint capacity.

The returning group was missing some familiar faces, including the first two players to reach 100 caps for the Ospreys, Barry Williams and Shaun Connor.

Connor had switched to the Dragons, while Williams had opted to retire after an injury-hit twelve months that had seen him undergo surgery on three separate occasions. The first captain to lift silverware for the region, Williams expressed his disappointment at having to hang up his boots:

> It's a very sad day for me. It's one that all professional sportsmen dread but unfortunately it seems that now is the appropriate time for me to hang up my boots. My body has been through a hell of a lot during my playing career and the wear and tear is finally catching up with me, I simply can't do another season. I have another

Sean Holley prepares to lead the Ospreys into action as the search for a replacement for Lyn Jones continues…

year left on my contract so I could have just sat on that and taken the wages for another twelve months but that goes against everything I believe in. I've enjoyed a fantastic career with plenty of highs that I'll be able to look back on, but undoubtedly, it's been an honour to have led the Ospreys during the early days.

Another player retiring was veteran centre and Grand Slam winner Mark Taylor, bringing the curtain down

on a distinguished career that had seen him play more than 50 times for Wales and tour with the Lions. Also leaving were wingers Aled Brew and Richard Mustoe, with the latter best remembered at the Liberty for his try in the famous win over Australia.

Key arrivals for the new season saw highly-rated Ireland wing Tommy Bowe joining, along with New Zealand 'A' scrum half Jamie Nutbrown from Crusaders, a direct replacement for compatriot Justin Marshall who had reached agreement with the region for an early contract release enabling him to sign for French club Montpellier.

One interesting temporary departure saw young centre Jonathan Spratt heading to New Zealand to play for Taranaki on loan in the Air NZ Cup, a switch organised by Andrew Hore.

Travelling in the opposite direction was Super 14 coach Ian Foster, who arrived in Ospreylia during August to provide guidance to the young coaching team while the search for a Head Coach continued. Waikato Chiefs coach Foster spent three weeks working with Holley and Humphreys, although Hore was quick to stress that Foster wasn't himself in the frame for the Ospreys job, saying: "His trip here is an agreed initiative between the Ospreys and the NZRU which will prove mutually beneficial, as not only will he be passing on his knowledge to our young coaches and assisting with their development, but he will also get to experience a new rugby culture."

There was a noticeable change at the Liberty Stadium over the summer when the outdated Neath Swansea Ospreys logo at the main entrance was replaced by the familiar mask logo, measuring 4.9m by 4.6m.

It had already replaced the old logo on the jersey the previous season, and the move was hailed as significant by Roger Blyth for highlighting how far the region had come in just five years.

Preparations for the new campaign gathered pace with two warm-up fixtures before the start of the new Magners campaign.

Leicester Tigers provided the first opposition of the summer in a testimonial match for winger Shane Williams, to mark ten years of service to rugby in the region, and they spoiled the party as they headed home with a 30–17 win in the bag.

Next it was a short trip up the Llynfi Valley to face a Regional Select XV, made up

Ian Evans tries to find a way through against Perpignan

Andrew Bishop tries to find a way through

of players from the four Premiership clubs in the region, Aberavon, Bridgend, Neath and Swansea, at Maesteg RFC.

While it was a huge public relations success with a large crowd of locals turning out to greet the region, the coaches would have learned very little from a one-sided affair, the Ospreys running in nine unanswered tries on their way to a 66–0 win.

September saw the new Magners campaign kick off with a busy month of five games scheduled, the first of them an away trip to Connacht, where a Nikki Walker try helped end the home team's proud record of having won the opening game of every Celtic League season to date, with eleven points from James Hook on top giving the Ospreys a 16–3 win.

Just four days later came the first Welsh derby of the season with Cardiff Blues visiting the Liberty Stadium, where an early Shane Williams try set the Ospreys on their way to a resounding 32–10 success over the capital city region. James Hook scored 22 points, including two tries, with new signing Tommy Bowe also touching down for his first try in the black shirt.

The positive start to the season continued with a 21–18 win in Glasgow, Alun Wyn Jones scoring in the final minute to pinch victory, and although the Ospreys suffered a first defeat of the season in Leinster, 19–13, they ended September with a stunning 43–0 hammering of Ulster at the Liberty. The Ospreys ran in six tries as they outclassed their opponents, to take top spot in the table.

Despite the positive start to the campaign, early season crowds at the Liberty Stadium were worryingly down on previous years, leading Ospreys directors to issue a stark warning on the future of the game.

"The expectation from supporters, and indeed, the desire from within the Ospreys, is to compete with the leading English and French clubs," they said. However, the warning came that "the reality is that we can only do this if we are getting the numbers through the turnstiles."

On the field, the team began their defence of the EDF Energy Cup on the first weekend of October with a home tie against Harlequins. Captain Ryan Jones had said pre-match that the Ospreys needed to win their first game, pointing out that the three-match structure of the competition meant defeat could see their trophy defence ended before they'd even got started, and it was a close run affair as Hook had to convert a 78th minute Bowe try to secure a 24–23 win.

The following two weekends were Heineken Cup fixtures, with the first game at Welford Road against Leicester Tigers. It proved a difficult afternoon, with the Ospreys defence having to be at its best to repel wave after wave of Leicester pressure, but the hosts eventually secured a 12–6 win to give them the early advantage in the pool.

Next up were Perpignan at the Liberty Stadium, and it seemed that supporters had heeded the directors' strong words as a season high crowd in excess of 10,000 turned out to watch the Ospreys win 15–9.

The two Heineken Cup fixtures had been played out against the backdrop of disciplinary action being taken against Gavin Henson, which saw bosses at the Ospreys impose a two-match ban on him following what was termed 'a rugby-related internal disciplinary decision'.

The ban should have seen the player sit out both Heineken Cup games, but a raft of injuries in the backline, including the late withdrawal of James Hook from the Perpignan game, left Holley and Humphreys with little option but to select Henson as a replacement rather than going into the game a man light.

Although he was an unused sub in that game, he was back in the starting XV for a 37–22 win over Worcester in the EDF a week later, scoring one of the Ospreys four tries. It was a result which meant that the losing bonus point they picked up in the next game, a 23–19 away defeat against London Irish, was enough to secure a third consecutive semi-final spot.

An incredible 16 Ospreys were named in Wales coach Warren Gatland's autumn international squad, while in typical Welsh rugby fashion, politics were never far away from the spotlight as the four regions united to announce the formation of Regional Rugby Wales, a new organisation to represent them as a unified body in all competitions or Union led negotiations moving forward.

With a three-week gap between fixtures, rumours began to emerge from the southern hemisphere that an end was in sight to the ongoing search for a new main man to lead the team, with reports suggesting that All Blacks backs coach, Wayne Smith, had been approached, and that he had rejected the post.

In a statement Ospreys management – who to this point had remained tight-lipped on the search for a new coach – confirmed only that Smith was just one of a number of individuals they were speaking to, and that these discussions should "provide an insight into the calibre of individual the Ospreys are prepared to engage with".

With Holley and Humphreys still at the helm, the team were defeated in Edinburgh at the end of November, 32–16, but then bounced back in style to secure two bonus point victories over Italian side Benetton Treviso in a Heineken Cup double-header, including a record Ospreys win, 68–8, in the home tie.

The usual busy Christmas schedule saw the Ospreys win two of three Welsh derbies. They picked up a losing bonus point at Rodney Parade in a 30–24 defeat to the Dragons, before only the third ever Liberty Stadium capacity crowd of 20,520 watched on Boxing Day as the Ospreys defeated the Scarlets 20–6. The festive period was then rounded off on New Year's Eve with a 16–12 win over Cardiff Blues, a late try from Filo Tiatia ensuring they ended 2008 at the top of the table.

A home defeat began 2009 as Munster left the Liberty with the points after a 25–21 win, on the day that speculation was again rife about the identity of any potential new Ospreys appointment. The name of former Wales coach Scott Johnson had come to the fore but, not for the first time since the departure of Lyn Jones, Ospreys bosses kept their own counsel.

The return of the Heineken Cup saw the Ospreys travel to Perpignan, where they had to settle for a losing bonus point after going down 17–15, a late rally almost being enough to clinch an unlikely win as they looked set to overturn a 17–0 deficit.

The defeat meant that the Ospreys' European fate went down to the final pool game, against Leicester a week later. Win and deny the Tigers a losing bonus point, and they would top the group. Anything else and the best they could hope for was a best runners-up spot behind their opponent.

It was a tight, rugged contest, with all the points coming from the boot; James Hook's five penalties giving the Ospreys a 15–9 win. It was a result that meant that Leicester went through, leaving the hosts hanging on until the following day for confirmation of their own progression to the last eight after results elsewhere went their way. Their reward, if it could be called that, was an away tie versus Munster.

The progression of both teams was marred slightly by a war of words post-match, with allegations of gouging from the Ospreys, claims vehemently denied by the Leicester camp. An investigation eventually led to Leicester captain Martin Corry cited for, and found guilty of, making contact with the eye area of Richard Hibbard.

The following week came confirmation of what was, by now, the worst kept secret in Welsh rugby, with the appointment of Scott Johnson to the new role of Director of Coaching at the Ospreys.

Johnson would be serving out a three-month notice period in his current post at the head of USA Rugby before arriving at the region to head up the team, working with Sean Holley (confirmed as Head Coach) and Jonathan Humphreys. In the meantime, the young Welsh duo would continue to lead a team pursuing silverware on three fronts.

Andrew Hore revealed that more than 20 coaches had been considered before settling on Johnson, who he had worked with previously as part of Wales' 2005 Grand Slam winning management team. Key to the appointment, he said, was Johnson's ability to develop young coaches, which fitted into the Ospreys ethos of development from within.

For his part, Johnson welcomed what he considered "a career defining experience", saying: "The challenges are clear and so are the goals; working alongside the coaching team to help move the Ospreys to a new stage of its development on the pitch and driving the support systems to bring through a steady stream of home grown players and coaches."

In the meantime though, it was business as usual for Holley and Humphreys as they maintained control of the team while they awaited Johnson's arrival.

Johnson wasn't the only southern hemisphere arrival confirmed, as Samoa captain Filipo Levi was brought in during February on a short-term deal to strengthen the pack for a busy end of season run-in.

Connacht were defeated 22–10 at the Liberty in the only game of February, before Leinster went home with the spoils after picking up a 13–8 win in Ospreylia at the start of March.

By the time 16 internationals returned from Six Nations duty two weeks later, the Ospreys were focussed on a big push for the final two months of the season. With the team in the knockout stages of two cups and still in with an outside chance of regaining their league title, there was still everything to play for under Holley and Humphreys.

First up was an EDF Energy Cup semi-final against Gloucester at Coventry's Ricoh Arena. The Ospreys status as current holders and finalists for the last two years counted for little though as they crashed out of the competition in an undignified manner, losing a dour contest, 17–0.

It was the first time in their short history that the Ospreys had been 'nilled', a statistic that didn't truly reflect the pattern of a game which they dominated for long periods without ever looking as though they possessed the firepower to break down stubborn but limited opponents.

Sean Holley was clearly downbeat after such a defeat, but he backed his team to respond accordingly with the European Cup quarter-final against Munster looming large on the horizon.

"What better game to have to try and put things right?" he asked. "We've got plenty to work on but we know that we have the ability in this squad to go to Munster and do well."

The Ospreys would have to do it without the services of Gavin Henson though, after he limped out of the first half of the Gloucester defeat with an ankle injury. Nobody knew it at the time, but it was to be the last time he was ever seen in an Ospreys shirt.

Before the Munster game there was the small matter of a Magners League fixture in Ulster, the Ospreys picking up a morale boosting 16–13 win.

Limerick welcomed the Ospreys on Easter Sunday, the day of the greatest of all miracles. No-one for one minute thought the Ospreys would require a similar miracle to secure a first ever Heineken Cup semi-final, but they were very much the underdogs going into the clash against the former champions.

It started well enough, James Hook and Ronan O'Gara exchanging penalties as Munster led 9–6 shortly before the break. However, a yellow card for Filo Tiatia proved the turning point, as a Paul Warwick try late in the first half took Munster clear for the first time.

Although Hook kept his side in touch with an early second-half penalty, Munster tails were up and a tired looking Ospreys side simply couldn't match their opponents who totally dominated, eventually winning 43–9.

It was a demoralising defeat, described by Ryan Jones as "an awfully difficult pill to swallow", while Sean Holley was at a loss to explain the second-half performance, saying:

> The only thing I can say is that today we were taught a lot of lessons and came second best in every facet of the game, on and off the field... We've been well beaten by a champion team. It's been a very painful experience. We went into a quarter-final with huge hopes. We've prepared the best that we can. Fair play to them, they ran away with it.

From challenging on three fronts, all that was left for the Ospreys now was the Magners League, and after two defeats of such magnitude the question was always going to be how they lifted themselves for the final five games of the season.

With almost perfect timing, Scott Johnson was unveiled to the media within a week of the Munster defeat. Although he would not be formally taking over until the end of the season, he would be spending the final weeks of the season acting in an observational capacity as he got to grips with the challenge that lay ahead.

He acknowledged that recent disappointments had made the challenge an even more difficult one, but he vowed to do his part to "help the Ospreys reach their full potential".

Managing Director Mike Cuddy laid out in clear and unambiguous terms what the expectation on Johnson was:

Richard Hibbard is held up agonisingly close as the Ospreys try to chip away at stubborn Gloucester defence in the EDF semi-final

The final whistle at Thomond Park and the Ospreys are out of the Heineken Cup

Our recent performance has been extremely disappointing; we have underachieved and failed to live up to our potential. Scott's arrival is extremely timely. We had previously identified where the organisation needed to be strengthened and his appointment is a part of a much wider plan aimed at re-establishing and enhancing the Ospreys' on-pitch performance.

Johnson's presence, watching from the stands as the Ospreys made their first ever visit to the new Parc y Scarlets stadium the following day, seemed to have a positive effect, the region winning 28–19 with tries from Ryan Jones, Shane Williams and Lee Byrne.

In truth though, what had been a season of real promise petered out over the closing weeks as the

Scott Johnson arrives in Ospreylia as Director of Coaching

Ospreys failed to find the consistency which had served them so well earlier.

A disappointing defeat at home to Edinburgh meant that despite back-to-back victories at the Liberty over the Dragons and Glasgow, the Ospreys title hopes were long gone by the time they returned to the site of their Easter heartbreak, Thomond Park, for the final game of the season. It was a similar story as Munster won 36–10 with a clinical performance, underlining exactly why they had secured a second Magners League title.

As they were presented with their trophy the Ospreys players looked on in envy, wondering how a season that had promised so much fell apart so badly in the final two months.

The incoming Scott Johnson spoke positively from the sidelines, giving hope for the following season, saying: "The reality is we've got a bit to work on but I think we've got a good enough player base to say we can work on it and get a good side."

The question on everybody's lips was could Johnson deliver on his promise and ensure the Ospreys did reach their full potential in 2009/10?

7

With Scott Johnson now firmly settled in and ready to take control for the first time expectations were rising ahead of 2009/10.

That expectation was heightened by the arrival of a true legend of the game, All Black Jerry Collins signing a two-year deal and arriving in Ospreylia after failing to settle in France where he had played for Toulon.

There were a handful of other new signings to help increase squad depth, the most significant being former Scarlet and once-capped Wales full-back, Barry Davies, while Tom Isaacs, a Sevens World Cup winner with Wales just months previously, arrived from Newport RFC.

A busy summer of international rugby saw Ospreys players travelling the globe, with six on the Lions tour to South Africa, ten named for Wales' games against USA and Canada, along with a sizable contingent in the U20 squad at the Junior World Championship in Japan, where a young flanker called Justin Tipuric finished second in the try-scoring charts with six in five games.

One player also missing from training was Gavin Henson, still suffering with a groin injury from the previous season's defeat to Gloucester in the EDF Energy Cup semi-final. Speculation was rife that the player was set to retire, a claim denied by both Henson and Mike Cuddy, although after initially reporting back for pre-season training, the player was granted indefinite leave by Ospreys management as he attempted to deal with his ongoing injury problems.

Pre-season form was promising as the Ospreys defeated two sides from the English Premiership. Leeds were beaten 35–20 at the Liberty Stadium while the following weekend they came from behind to defeat Gloucester at Kingsholm 22–16.

There was one big change to the Magners League this season. Following in the footsteps of other major competitions, including the English Premiership, France's T14 and Super Rugby in the southern hemisphere, the league winners would now be decided via an end of season play-off, with the first target to finish in the top four at the end of the regular season.

For teams like the Ospreys who regularly provided a disproportionate number of players to the national set-up, this was a welcome change that allowed them to remain competitive despite the obvious handicap of their international contribution at certain times of the season.

With spirits buoyed following a good pre-season the first competitive fixture of the Johnson era was one with the potential to burst any bubble, a difficult away trip to Connacht. However, on a typical wet and windy Galway night, a debut try from Jerry Collins helped his new team to a winning start to the season as they came out on top 19–12.

The opening month of the campaign was a frustrating one though, despite the optimism in the camp, as the first-day win was followed by back-to-back home defeats on consecutive weekends, 20–16 against Ulster and 18–11 against Leinster.

Having expected a better start to the season, supporters weren't slow in voicing their feelings after the second defeat, a chorus of boos overshadowing the final whistle. Sean Holley acknowledged that fans had a right to let the team know how they felt, but urged them to stick with the team as nothing is won or lost in the opening weeks.

> We're in the entertainment business and we didn't entertain tonight. People are paying good money to watch us and we have to improve. It was a poor performance so we probably deserved to get booed off. I'm disappointed about the fact that we haven't impressed our supporters, there's nobody more disappointed than me, I want to win more than anybody else... We're pretty disappointed but not down and out. We've got a long way to go, you don't win anything in September.

A positive reaction was needed, and that was what the coaches got. First up was Glasgow away where 20 unanswered second-half points gave the Ospreys a 26–16 win. That was followed by a 31–10 success over Edinburgh at the Liberty, with tries from Tommy Bowe, Ryan Jones, Lee Byrne and Jonathan Thomas, which left the Magners League table looking a lot healthier from an Ospreys point of view as they switched focus to the Heineken Cup and headed to Welford Road for what promised to be a tough afternoon against Leicester Tigers.

What materialised was an enthralling contest that saw the Ospreys build up an 18-point first-half lead before being pegged back with both teams eventually having to settle for a share of the spoils at 32 apiece.

The draw meant the Ospreys headed home with two points, Leicester claiming an extra bonus point after scoring four tries, but as try scorer Shane Williams pointed out post-match, despite the disappointment at letting the win slip, a draw meant the team were ahead of where they had been twelve months previously after a round one defeat at the same venue: "We're in a better position than we were last year, we've come up to Leicester and taken two points from an away fixture and Leicester have dropped points from a home fixture, so that's a bit of an advantage to us."

The following week saw French giants Clermont Auvergne come to the Liberty, and as is always the case in European competition, the pressure was on to secure a home win or face the prospect of an early elimination.

It was a similar story to the previous weekend as the Ospreys raced into a 22–3 half-time lead thanks to tries from Tommy Bowe, Ryan Jones and Barry Davies, only for their opponents to rally after the break, scoring 21 points in the third quarter to nudge ahead. Thankfully, on this occasion the Ospreys were able to come again, Dan Biggar's penalty restoring the lead before dogged defence saw them hold on to a valuable 25–24 win.

There was disappointment in the next two Magners League games, a 20–12 derby defeat away to Cardiff Blues followed by a 9–9 draw at home to Glasgow, the latter fixture coming as the Ospreys were without ten players on Wales duty for the autumn series and a further 15 on the injured list.

A quieter November, which saw just two games in the new-look Anglo-Welsh Cup, a downgraded development competition called the LV= Cup, allowed coaches and fans alike to look at some of the young talent coming through the ranks. Despite defeats to Northampton (19–17) and Bath (21–11), there were first Ospreys calls for the likes of Justin Tipuric, Hanno Dirksen and James King, players who would go on in future seasons to become key players for the region.

By the time December arrived, although the Ospreys were able to welcome back their international contingent, a growing injury list was becoming an increasing concern, forcing the region to bring in reinforcements.

Former Cardiff Blues second row James Goode signed after returning to Wales from New Zealand where he had been playing in the Air NZ Cup. Meanwhile, with all three Heineken Cup registered scrum halves struggling with long-term injuries, South African international Ricky Januarie agreed a three-month loan deal from his Super Rugby province, Stormers.

Despite the injuries, Munster were seen off 19–14 at the Liberty Stadium in the Magners League, before a European double-header against Italian side Viadana on back-to-back weekends.

The first leg at Stadio Giglio saw Januarie making his debut less than 24 hours after meeting his new colleagues for the first time, after flying straight to Italy from South Africa, and with just one light training session under his belt. Nevertheless he made a huge

impact, scoring one of eight Ospreys tries as he steered the team to a convincing 62–7 win.

Another player with good cause to remember that game was teenager Tom Prydie, from Porthcawl, who made his competition debut off the bench in the second half to become the youngest ever player to appear in the Heineken Cup, aged 17 years and 293 days.

Although something of a foregone conclusion, there was still a job to be done in the return match a week later, and it was a satisfactory afternoon's work as the Ospreys ran in six tries to win 45–19, leaving them very much in contention for the knockout stages.

Christmas then saw the usual festive derbies, and the Ospreys rounded off an unbeaten December with a Boxing Day defeat of the Scarlets, a 21–14 win courtesy of an unlikely brace of tries from prop Paul James, before starting 2010 with a resounding 26–0 thumping of the Blues at the Liberty Stadium on New Year's Day.

The following week should have seen the Ospreys make the trip to Ulster, but a frozen Ravenhill pitch meant that the game had to be postponed, a decision which would have at the time unseen ramifications for the region during an eventful second half of the season.

Because of this the Ospreys were forced to travel to France for the return clash against Clermont Auvergne without a game in two weeks, and despite taking an early lead through a Tommy Bowe try they were decidedly second best in all areas as the French side took control of pool three with a 27–7 win.

The setback meant the following weekend's home game against Leicester was now a do-or-die affair. As Ryan Jones said post-match in France: "We were up

Young flanker Justin Tipuric marks his first senior start with his first Ospreys try

against the best team in France today and we came up short, we have to make sure that next week we stand up to, and match, the best team in England."

In the region's short history they had already enjoyed some momentous tussles against the Tigers. This one was to top the lot, on and off the field.

On the field, a Tommy Bowe try proved the difference as the Ospreys won 17–12 to secure a place in the final eight for a third consecutive season,

eliminating Leicester in the process after a nail biting contest.

There were joyous celebrations at the final whistle, but the main talking point of the game came as the match moved into the last ten minutes and it wasn't a try, a tackle or a scrum.

Lee Byrne had been forced off with a blood injury after damaging a toe, to be replaced temporarily by Sonny Parker. When Byrne returned to the field a few minutes later, seemingly without seeking permission from the officials, confusion reigned as no player exited.

The Ospreys briefly had 16 players on the pitch, Parker stepped off field on the far side and Byrne didn't know whether to stay on or come off, forcing the referee Allan Lewis to halt proceedings and clarify the situation. Eventually, it was sorted, Byrne returning officially, with Parker heading back to the bench, and that, so the Ospreys thought, was that.

Immediately after the game Leicester officials, furious at seeing their team eliminated, lodged a complaint with ERC regarding the 16th man incident. The worst-case scenario could see the team thrown out of the competition and Leicester reinstated. The whole of Ospreylia held its breath.

Although the draw for the quarter-finals took place as scheduled and handed the Ospreys an away tie against Biarritz, behind the scenes investigations were continuing and it was confirmed by ERC that they were bringing charges against both Byrne and the Ospreys.

As 16 players departed for Six Nations duty, including Byrne, a new-look coaching team led by Jonathan Humphreys took the region back into LV= Cup duty, the Ospreys using the developmental side of the competition to benefit young coaches as well as players.

On the same day as the Ospreys were well beaten at the Dragons in the LV=, 40–19, came news of an ERC disciplinary verdict.

It was held that the player had returned to the field without permission, despite knowing that he needed permission. It was a clear breach of protocol said ERC, and the club should have done more to prevent it.

The verdict was guilty but the view of the panel,

much to the relief of the region, was that it had not been pre-meditated and there had been no material effect on the outcome. As such, the penalty was a 25,000 Euro fine for the Ospreys, with the player suspended for two weeks, a ban he successfully appealed against.

The Ospreys were still in the Cup!

February saw the Ospreys, minus their internationals, win two from two at the Liberty, against Leeds in the LV= Cup and Connacht in the Magners, but behind the scenes two disputes continued to rumble on which threatened to derail the season.

First, ERC launched a second investigation into the Ospreys, this time regarding issues surrounding the registration of Ricky Januarie – who by now had left Ospreylia and headed back to South Africa – on a short-term contract. Then, the Ospreys found themselves in dispute with Celtic Rugby and Ulster, over the proposed date for the rearranged fixture following January's postponement.

Eventually, ERC found in the Ospreys favour, but in the case of the row over the Ulster fixture, the parties couldn't agree on a new date, with the Ospreys unwilling to schedule it for March during the Six Nations.

The Ospreys argued that they simply didn't have enough front row players available for the rearranged date, due to international call-ups and injuries, insisting that the fixture should be scheduled for a date to be agreed post Six Nations.

Meanwhile, Edinburgh recorded a thumping win over the Ospreys at Murrayfield, 33–17, before confirmation came that the Ulster game would be played midweek in

Scott Johnson briefs Ricky Januarie after the scrum half met up with his team-mates in Italy just hours ahead of a crunch Heineken Cup tie

April, between the Heineken Cup game against Biarritz and an away Magners game versus Leinster.

Defeat at Rodney Parade to the Dragons at the end of the month, 28–20, made it two losses from two in March, but a 27–19 win over the Scarlets meant that the Ospreys were well placed for the end of season run-in and a potential place in the first ever Magners Grand Final.

Next up was the big Heineken Cup quarter-final clash with Biarritz. The Basque team had moved the

Even international rugby players have to queue for their luggage at the airport…

game just across the French/Spanish border to San Sebastian, where it would be played in front of a sell-out 25,000 crowd at Estadio Anoeta, home of the town's professional football club, Real Sociedad.

Those present were to witness an incredible game, but one that ultimately proved a heartbreaking experience for the 1,000 plus travelling Ospreys fans.

They watched their team slug it out toe-to-toe with their opponents, outscoring the French side three tries to two as Ryan Jones, Lee Byrne and Nikki Walker all touched down. Trailing 16–15 at the break, there was still only a point separating the teams at the final whistle as Biarritz held on to win 29–28. The defeat saw the Ospreys eliminated for the third successive season at this stage.

Speaking after the match, Shane Williams spoke for everyone when he said:

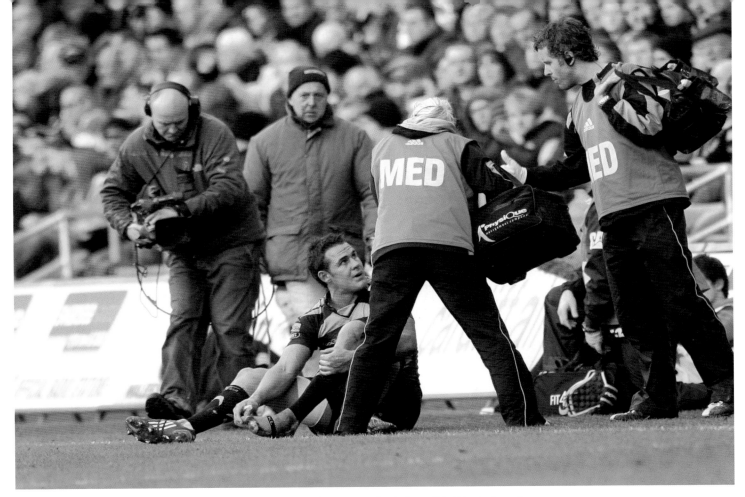

Lee Byrne received treatment for a bloodied toe on the Liberty Stadium turf — before all hell broke loose!

We are really gutted that we have come this far, worked so hard to get there but are going home again with nothing. We scored some good tries and should have won the game but that's no consolation... I thought we had them but it's another loss. We had worked our guts out to get out of a very strong group and into this position. You don't mind losing if you deserve it but this was different. That's what's so hard to take.

There was no time at all to dwell on the loss though as the team had to head straight to Ireland for back-to-back Magners game. The rearranged clash with Ulster was first up, just four days later, a game given even more spice with the news in the build-up of a Celtic Rugby disciplinary hearing over the Ospreys refusal to play on the rearranged March date.

With just four games to go there was no margin for error, and the response from the Biarritz disappointment was the perfect one, running in four tries to secure a bonus point in a 38–27 win that moved them into second place.

Seventy-two hours later they found themselves in Dublin to face Leinster, and although they lost that one 20–16, a losing bonus point meant that they could be relatively content with their week-long stay in Ireland.

After a few days rest and recuperation the team were back in the Emerald Isle a week later for the penultimate fixture of the regular season, with 15 points from the boot of Dan Biggar enough to secure a crucial win over Munster.

An Ulster win in Edinburgh the following day guaranteed the Ospreys a home semi-final for finishing in second place, rendering the outcome of the final game, against the Dragons at the Liberty, irrelevant. Nevertheless, the Ospreys were in rampant form, picking up a bonus point with a 42–10 win.

Glasgow were the visitors for the semi-final a week later, and the day before the game, Celtic Rugby passed judgement on the Ulster affair, fining the Ospreys £100,000 and imposing a four-point deduction on the team for the following season. It was a verdict that infuriated Glasgow officials; an immediate four-point penalty would have seen the fixture switched with Glasgow now the home team.

With added spice to the game, the two teams went head to head in the first ever Magners League play-off match, but in truth the Ospreys made light work of their opponents. They continued their excellent run of form to win 20–5, booking their place in the first Grand Final. Their opponents would be Leinster, who saw off Munster to secure home rights in the final.

The Ospreys headed to Dublin at the end of May in good form but seen as the underdogs by most observers. They had never won at Leinster's RDS Showground home, a venue where the hosts were unbeaten in the Magners League for over two years.

After a fast and frenetic opening, however, it was the Ospreys fans in a capacity crowd that were cheering first as Tommy Bowe took advantage of some great play by Andrew Bishop to get the first try, which was converted

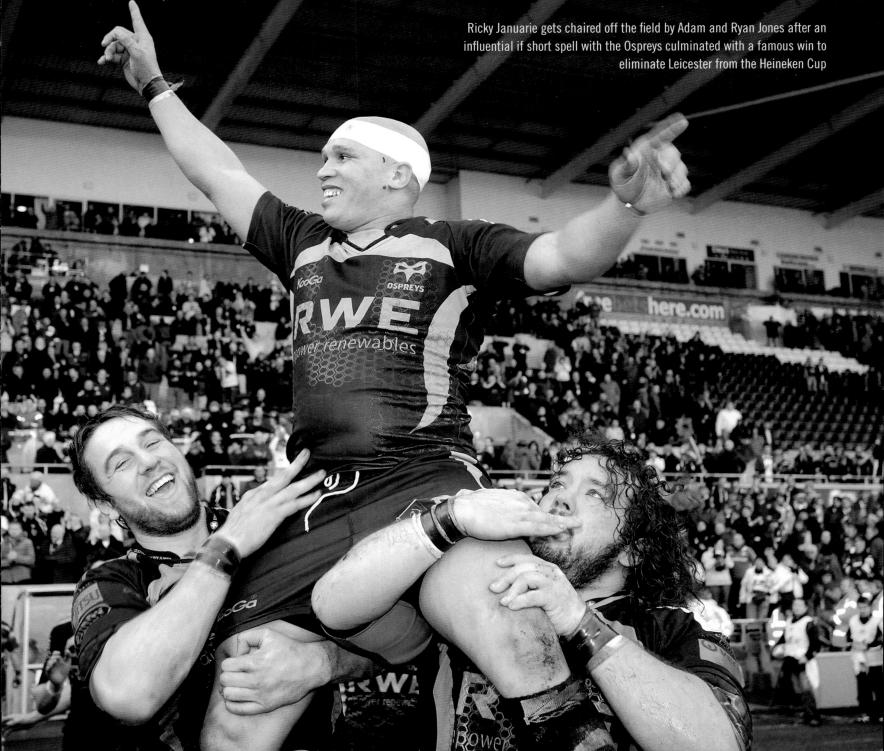

Ricky Januarie gets chaired off the field by Adam and Ryan Jones after an influential if short spell with the Ospreys culminated with a famous win to eliminate Leicester from the Heineken Cup

Ryan Jones scores an early try for the Ospreys against Biarritz

by Biggar. James Hook then crossed for a second score, giving the Ospreys a 14–3 lead at the break.

As you'd expect, Leinster threw absolutely everything at the Ospreys in the second half, desperate to claw their way back into the game, but they were restricted to just three more penalties as the visitors held on for an historic 17–12 win, becoming the first side to claim three Celtic League titles in the process.

Post-match, Sean Holley argued that the manner of the win was the perfect riposte to critics of the Ospreys, saying:

Disbelief at the final whistle against Biarritz as the Ospreys miss out on a place in the last four

Without wanting to sound cocky, we do feel that we've got what we deserved, we've played some good rugby this year and we've worked really hard as a group. That's four trophies in seven years; it's not a bad strike rate. We get very little credit for it; we're seen as something that we think we're not. In adversity, some times the character comes out and that's what you've seen with the Ospreys this year.

Skipper Ryan Jones proudly looked back at the period after the Biarritz defeat as key to the title success:

Redemption for Lee Byrne after the 16th man controversy as he crosses for the second try in the Grand Final at the RDS

The Magners League champions celebrate

We can look back at that week in Ireland after the Biarritz game as crucial. We played three games in six or seven days, at this level it's incredibly tough. What your body goes through, and what you go through emotionally it's tough. But the boys came out of that superbly and it stood us in good stead for the rest of the season. It's something that we weathered and we grew tighter as a group. I think it was good for us in the long run.

The questions on most observers' lips were could the Ospreys build on this win and not only defend their crown, but make that next step in Europe and reach the last four?

8

For the Ospreys' 14-strong contingent named in the summer Wales touring party to face South Africa and New Zealand, there was little time to celebrate their latest league success as they went straight into international duty within days of the win in Leinster.

After a month off, however, the core group returned to Llandarcy at the start of July ready to defend their title.

Change to the squad was minimal; fans' favourite Filo Tiatia bowed out, his appearance in the final the previous season proving to be his 99th and last one as he hung up his playing boots at the age of 39 to take up a coaching role.

Wing Jonny Vaughton was the most notable other playing departure after 63 appearances for the region, including the win over Australia and the 2008 EDF Cup final victory at Twickenham.

Off the field, Paul Thorburn parted company with the organisation after four years in a commercial role at the Liberty Stadium.

Coming through the arrivals door were veteran hooker Mefin Davies, re-signing from Leicester almost six years after his last appearance for the region, Dragons wing Richard Fussell, Blues fly-half Dai Flanagan and young number eight Morgan Allen from Newport RFC.

After such an enthralling end to the previous campaign it was evident that the coaching team were fairly satisfied with where the group were at, looking to tweak rather than overhaul the squad during pre-season.

There was one additional departure, with the sad confirmation that Ospreys 'original' Lyndon Bateman was to hang up his boots after conceding defeat in his long-term battle to overcome a knee injury 18 months earlier. A double Celtic League winner who played in the win over Australia, Bateman made 79 Ospreys appearances, scoring two tries.

A Regional Select XV, drawn from the five Premiership clubs in Ospreylia and led by highly rated Aberavon coach, Simon King, provided the first pre-season opposition of the summer in front of a healthy crowd at the Talbot Athletic Ground.

Unsurprisingly, a youthful Ospreys team were pretty much untroubled as they enjoyed a 58–22 win, running in nine tries. The win came at a cost though, as centre Jonathan Spratt suffered damage to knee ligaments on his return to action after six months sidelined through a disc problem, and would ultimately miss the entire season after undergoing surgery.

There was no rest for the Ospreys though, who hit the road to face English Premiership opposition Leeds just four days later, via a two-day stop in north Wales. It proved to be a tough affair and just the test that the coaches would have wanted as Leeds raced into 22–9 lead before a late rally secured the win, a team still without its large international contingent showing great character as tries from Fussell, James King, and Welsh Guardsman Matthew Dwyer, secured a 31–28 win.

The final warm-up game saw Gloucester come out on top 24–14 at a wet Liberty Stadium after a performance that left Scott Johnson saying: "There was some good, there was some bad and there was some ugly. We had a bit of it all out there really didn't we?"

There were two weeks for the charismatic Aussie to iron out the issues ahead of the season curtain-raiser, the always difficult trip to Ravenhill to face Ulster.

Ahead of that game it was announced that second row Alun Wyn Jones would lead the team into the new season after being named as captain, replacing namesake Ryan who had held the post for the last three years.

The outgoing skipper was magnanimous as he handed over the armband, saying: "I've always said that captaincy is a seat that you are keeping warm for someone else. I've done it to the best of my ability at all times, we've had highs and lows, and I've thoroughly enjoyed it. I think that Alun Wyn is a fantastic person and will make a great captain."

For his part, the new captain indicated that he wouldn't be afraid to turn to his colleague for assistance should it be needed:

> I come to work every day to learn and to improve, and I'm well aware that I don't have all the answers... I will turn up for work every day with the same attitude, regardless of being captain, and if I'm not learning there's no point in me being here. I'm not afraid to ask

for any help or to draw upon the vast experience around me in the squad.

The new campaign began with the Ospreys rooted to the foot of the table on minus four points as they waited on their appeal against the deduction handed out the previous season for failing to fulfil a fixture against Ulster.

Ironically, the new campaign got underway with a return visit to Ravenhill, where they suffered a bonus-point defeat against the Ulstermen, a late penalty from Niall O'Connor securing a 27–26 win for the home team.

The Magners League had been extended over the summer with the introduction of two Italians teams to the competition and the following weekend saw the first visit to the Liberty of an Italian team for a league match, when Benetton Treviso were the opposition, providing little by way of resistance as the Ospreys won 32–16 to secure a winning bonus point to kick-start their title defence.

There was a boost when it was confirmed that the appeal against the points deduction had been successful and the four points reinstated, Johnson describing the verdict as "justice prevailed".

The next two games followed a similar pattern, a 22–10 defeat on the road in Munster before collecting another bonus-point win over an Italian team at the Liberty Stadium as Aironi were defeated 38–6.

At the start of October a 21–18 defeat of the Scarlets, with Fussell and Alun Wyn Jones both scoring tries, gave the Ospreys their first away win of the season as they maintained their good record over their nearest rivals.

Nikki Walker in typically deadly form as Treviso come to the Liberty for the first time as a Magners League outfit

The focus then changed to the Heineken Cup, and first up was a trip to the Côte d'Azur in the south of France and Jonny Wilkinson's star-studded Toulon.

It was, as anticipated, a tight, close affair, all square at 6–6 at the break. However, the Ospreys gained control in the third quarter as Shane Williams took advantage of a Toulon knock-on to score the first try of the game.

With just six minutes to go, Wilkinson slotted over a penalty to bring his team back to within two points before he set up his fellow England cap, Paul Sackey, to score a match-winning try in the last four minutes. Wilkinson's conversion sealed a 19–16 success.

It was crucial that the Ospreys bounced straight back as the following weekend saw Aviva Premiership leaders London Irish at the Liberty and a win was essential to

To help promote the arrival of Italian teams into the Magners League, the Ospreys teamed up with Italian businesses across the region

ensure European hopes weren't over before they'd even got going.

A crowd of almost 12,500 were at the Liberty Stadium to see an early Tommy Bowe try and a typical piece of individual brilliance from Shane Williams secure an impressive 27–16 victory.

There was disappointment in the Magners however, with back-to-back defeats in the next two games, losing 31–23 at Glasgow despite a hat-trick from the Ospreys' Scottish wing Nikki Walker, while the following weekend

back at the Liberty the Dragons secured their first ever win in Ospreylia to end the home team's 14-month unbeaten home record in the competition. With the autumn international series starting just a week later, the Ospreys had been without 15 members of the Welsh squad.

Sandwiched between the two losses came confirmation from joint Managing Director, Mike Cuddy, that 18 months after his last regional appearance and more than a year after taking a sabbatical from rugby,

Gavin Henson was being released from his contract at the Ospreys in order to sign for Saracens.

On the field, a third straight defeat followed when the Ospreys went down 18–17 to Newcastle Falcons in the LV= Cup development competition, young fly-half Matthew Jarvis striking the upright with a penalty attempt to win the game late on.

Meanwhile another fly-half, James Hook, ended lengthy speculation about his future when he confirmed to regional management in early November that he would not be accepting the new contract offer that was on the table and would leave his home region at the end of the current season.

Next up was an historic day for the Ospreys as they took a competitive fixture to Bridgend for the very first time. Old foes Leicester were the visitors for an LV= Cup match that was the first regional game played at the Brewery Field, home of Bridgend Ravens, since the demise of the Celtic Warriors in 2004.

The decision to take the game on the road was made with the future development of the region in mind, to ensure that although their town was on the fringes of Ospreylia the people of Bridgend felt a part of their region.

Managing Director, Roger Blyth, said at the time: "I'm sure the rugby-loving public of Bridgend will turn out to back the Ospreys in numbers, in particular the local boys from that area who will be pulling on the shirt."

As it was, they turned out in their thousands in dreadful conditions to watch the Ospreys demolish the Tigers, making light of the heavy rain and muddy pitch to run in eight tries to win 46–13 in front of the Sky Sports cameras.

The switch was declared a success, with the Ospreys vowing to be back in Bridgend later in the season. Blyth commented post-match:

> We made the decision to bring this game to Bridgend based on a number of circumstances, and things have gone as well as we could possibly have imagined. The crowd was far bigger than either of our home LV= Cup matches last season, which in itself is vindication of the decision to play it at the Brewery Field... The people of Bridgend have turned out in numbers and really shown that they consider themselves to be Ospreys.

Although the international players were still away, it was back to Magners action for the Ospreys after defeats in their last two league games. Hard-fought wins over Connacht (16–15 away from home) and Leinster at the Liberty (19–15) steadied the ship before the visit of Edinburgh at the start of December.

It was to be a month of adverse wintry weather, with the UK hit by heavy snowfall, and Edinburgh managed to escape the worst of the early snow to arrive in south Wales for their Magners League date, but they returned home wishing they hadn't after being thumped 33–16 by an Ospreys team reinforced by the return of their Welsh international contingent.

The win put the Ospreys up into the top four for the first time in the season and was the perfect warm-up for the European double-header against Irish heavyweights, Munster.

Ahead of the first game in Thomond Park, the Ospreys had to successfully defend Marty Holah at a series of disciplinary hearings after he was cited for

Shane Williams leads the London Irish a merry dance on his way to a stunning solo try

tripping an opponent in the win over Edinburgh. A key member of the Ospreys pack, he was initially banned for two weeks, but following an appeal which was held on the Friday night, he was cleared to travel to Limerick the following day with the rest of the team for Sunday's match.

It was to prove a frustrating afternoon, despite Tommy Bowe's length of the field score putting his team ahead early in the second half, the match turning on a yellow card issued to Paul James just before the hour.

Munster took full advantage of the extra man to add 14 points during the ten minute sin-binning and although the hosts themselves played out the closing minutes a man light after their talisman Paul O'Connell was red carded for a forearm smash on Jonathan Thomas, it finished 22–16 to the home team.

The two teams would go at it again a week later, but first they had to overcome further bad weather with Ospreylia covered in two feet of snow the day before the return match. Under-soil heating ensured the pitch was playable and hard work to clear the areas surrounding the stadium meant that the game could go ahead.

Although more than 15,000 tickets had been sold for the game, travel problems meant that the attendance for the crunch games was actually down on that figure with just above 12,000 present.

A gutsy effort from the forwards provided the platform for a vital Ospreys win despite being outscored two to one on the try front, 14 points from Dan Biggar on top of a Mike Phillips try securing a 19–15 win which meant that there was just three points separating leaders Toulon, Munster and the Ospreys, with everything to play for in the final two rounds.

The wintry weather continued, and despite the Boxing Day derby against the Scarlets at the Liberty selling out prior to

Regional rugby returns to Bridgend

Dan Biggar and Tommy Bowe enjoy themselves as the Ospreys record a record victory over the Scarlets in the rearranged Christmas fixture

Christmas, the game unexpectedly fell foul of the conditions and was postponed just two hours ahead of kick-off.

On this occasion the pitch was perfect and there was no risk in the surrounding areas. Instead, frozen pipes caused by overnight temperatures of −10°c meant there was no running water available in two of the stands, forcing stadium management to make the unpopular decision.

Following several hours of discussions with all parties, the decision was made to play the game the following day, also a Bank Holiday. Given the short notice, the attendance was inevitably down from the capacity crowd expected.

Nevertheless, the Ospreys fans in the 18,151 attendance would have thoroughly enjoyed their belated Christmas rugby treat as their team not only made it six straight wins over their local rivals, they scored seven tries on their way to a record score-line against the Scarlets, winning 60–17.

However, they seemed to be suffering a festive hangover four days later when a sluggish start and poor first-half showing ultimately proved the difference as Cardiff Blues won 27–25 on New Year's Eve at the Cardiff City Stadium, the Ospreys unable to overturn a 21-point deficit despite a valiant late effort.

If one thing had characterised the season to date it was the Ospreys lack of consistency and their up and down form continued the following weekend with another loss, this time going down 15–10 away to Leinster.

A trip to London Irish for round five of the Heineken Cup offered a perfect opportunity to blow away the new year blues. Irish had been in dreadful form since losing at the Liberty Stadium back in October, a ten-game losing run seeing them slip down the Aviva Premiership table that they had topped at the time of visiting Ospreylia.

Most pundits were backing the Ospreys to bag the win that would take the hunt for a place in the last eight into the final round. But, on a disappointing afternoon at the Madejski Stadium, they failed to secure the victory which would have set up a winner takes all clash against Toulon at the Liberty the following weekend.

Irish led from the early stages, scoring two tries, and the Ospreys had no answer. They were well beaten, going down 24–12 to end their hopes of progression.

The challenge now for the Ospreys was to bounce back as they had after European disappointment the previous year.

The dead rubber at the Liberty the following weekend, against a much changed Toulon side, allowed the Ospreys to show their character, coming from 14–3 down early on to win 29–17, but that was the end of the road in the Heineken Cup for another season.

Back-to-back wins in the LV= Cup over the Blues and Wasps, the latter fixture marking a return to Bridgend for the region, lifted spirits but weren't enough to keep Ospreys interest in that competition alive either.

As the old saying goes, it was time to focus on the league once again, and the defence of their title. Minus the senior and U20 international contingent who were away on Six Nations duty, the Ospreys put together some of their best form of the season, following their two LV= wins with a further four straight wins in the Magners, to equal the region's record of seven consecutive victories.

Ulster were defeated 23–22 at the Liberty before Treviso were doubled, thanks to a 34–18 win in Italy. Home games against Connacht and Glasgow then provided comfortable victories, 33–18 and 37–6 respectively, with Ashley Beck scoring a try in the latter game that would be voted Magners League try of the season, to leave the Ospreys well in contention for the play-offs once more.

Off the field Andy Lloyd confirmed he would be retiring at the end of the season after being appointed Team Administrator in place of Dani Delamere who was moving to a role in the commercial department,

while James Hook's destination for the following season was revealed to be French club Perpignan.

There was further news of player departures when management at the region confirmed a deal with another French team, Clermont Auvergne, for the services of Lee Byrne, despite the full-back having another year on his contract.

Mike Cuddy explained: "We would not have seen much of Lee next season (a World Cup year), when he will be 31, and for him to have the security of a three-year contract and the change of lifestyle that this move will allow him, is a fantastic personal opportunity."

In other words, the Ospreys would have been paying a player who would have missed half of the season between World Cup and Six Nations duties in his final year, so it made little financial sense in what was a changing economic climate to fight to retain his services.

There was sad news when flanker Ben Lewis confirmed his retirement through injury in March, the 24-year-old failing to recover from a neck injury sustained in the win over Aironi at the Liberty earlier in the season. A week later, Irish second row Conor McInerney also hung up his boots because of ongoing knee problems.

While behind the scenes there was a clear balancing of the books taking place as the Ospreys looked to reshape its squad for the next season; there was the small matter of a top-four spot up for grabs with just five games remaining.

The first of those was on the road versus Edinburgh, where despite the welcome return of their international players, the Ospreys' winning run was abruptly halted as the Scots came out on top 23–16.

A week later Cardiff Blues visited the Liberty Stadium, where they held the Ospreys to a 21–21 draw in a dour affair that was dominated by the boot.

With just three games to go, the return to the stuttering form of earlier in the season had come at exactly the wrong time, but skipper Alun Wyn Jones urged his charges to rise to the challenge: "Nothing's changed for us

Mike Phillips tries to drive the misfiring Ospreys back-line as they exit the Heineken Cup with a defeat at London Irish

Fun and games with a young fan

with this result, we need to win all our remaining games and that's the aim in order to cement that top-four place. We're in third place now and we definitely need the points to freeze our place up there."

However, the first of those remaining games ended in disappointment as the Ospreys crashed to defeat at the hands of the Dragons, 32–28, having trailed 32–11 midway through the second half.

Defeat at home to Munster in the penultimate game of the regular season, Ronan O'Gara's three pointer with the last kick of the match clinching it 22–20 for the visitors, meant that play-off hopes were hanging in the balance.

As the business continued to wrestle with its finances amidst the ongoing global financial crisis, there was a surprise announcement in late April, Elite Performance Director Andrew Hore was named as Chief Operations Officer and took over responsibility for all day-to-day activities within the organisation, business and rugby.

He was tasked with the development and implementation of the long-term strategic plan for the overall business, as well as helping to develop systems and structures to improve financial performance.

Although an appointment that would have meant little to the supporters desperate to see the region book a play-off spot, it was an appointment which it was hoped would have a major impact on the off-field performance of the business, allowing the Ospreys to remain competitive for many years to come.

Going into the final day of the season the Ospreys lay one point and one place behind Cardiff Blues who held the fourth and final play-off spot, and travelled to Viadana to face Aironi knowing victory might still not be enough, but Dan Biggar wasn't throwing the towel in, saying:

> At the minute the table says that we are the fifth-best team in the league but there's one more game to go and a win in that could see us up to fourth and even third in the league after the full round of fixtures, and that will mean that we deserve to be in the play-offs… We aren't kidding ourselves that it's been a great season, and if results don't go for us on Friday then, again, the table

will reflect our true standing. It's very tight around the play-offs, that shows it's a competitive league.

It went right to the wire, but in the end a James Hook penalty with just four minutes of the season remaining secured that play-off spot for the Ospreys.

It was a far from vintage performance, just as it had been far from a vintage season, but Hook's penalty, after three from Biggar, secured a 12–10 win which meant that with the Scarlets defeating the Blues back in Wales, it was the Ospreys who finished fourth and would travel to face Munster in the play-offs the following weekend, the fifth game that season between the two teams.

In contrast to the previous year when the Ospreys had raced into the play-offs in top form, this time around they had stumbled over the line, and in many people's eyes they headed back to Thomond Park for the play-off semi-final more in hope than expectation, and so it played out.

Munster were dominant from start to finish, only some heroic defence against wave after wave of red attacks keeping the Ospreys in the game. In truth, the home team were comfortable victors, Fussell's late try merely adding a gloss of respectability to the final scoreline of 18–11.

The Ospreys bowed out, Munster going on to equal the region's record of three Celtic crowns two weeks later when they defeated Leinster at Thomond Park.

For the Ospreys, it had been a disappointing season on the field, and one of change off it. There was still plenty more change to come as Welsh rugby battled with its finances, but as the plane headed home from Limerick there was plenty for Ospreys management and players to think about.

Richard Hibbard spills blood for the cause in the play-off semi-final away to Munster

9

After the disappointing end to the previous season, there was something of an air of uncertainty around the place when the squad returned to Llandarcy ahead of the new campaign.

A number of high profile and big name players had departed Ospreylia over the summer, including Welsh internationals Lee Byrne, James Hook, Craig Mitchell, Mike Phillips and Jonathan Spratt, as well as All Black legends Jerry Collins and Marty Holah and their compatriot, Jamie Nutbrown, the Kiwi trio all returning home.

Coming in were Samoan duo George Stowers (who had been a destructive force for London Irish in their win over the Ospreys a few months earlier) and Kahn Fotuali'i, along with Canadian Chauncey O'Toole and Welsh qualified pair Aaron Jarvis from Bath and Joe Bearman (Dragons).

In addition, the Ospreys had bid farewell to two of the coaching staff as fans' favourite Filo Tiatia headed to Japan to take up a post with his former club Toyota Verblitz, while Skills Coach Gruff Rees joined Italian side Aironi in a similar role – although he was to return to Ospreylia in the not too distant future.

It's probably fair to say that the mood among the Ospreys support at this time wasn't the brightest.

Having seen so many favourites depart, online forums were predicting a long, hard season ahead for the region.

That feeling was exacerbated when Wales coach Warren Gatland named his squad for the forthcoming Rugby World Cup with eight Ospreys included, meaning they could miss the first two months of the season, while the three new overseas recruits were also confirmed as being involved in New Zealand, along with Tommy Bowe in the green of Ireland.

While supporters may have had their doubts, behind the scenes the Ospreys management genuinely believed that the direction they were taking the organisation was the right one, and was one that would reap rewards.

Having been stuck with the 'galacticos' label, somewhat unfairly, the region had taken conscious action to rid itself of a tag that had always irked somewhat, feeling that it never truly reflected what the team were about and, even worse, had actively detracted local supporters from being able to identify with and buy into the cause.

In the face of inflated salaries caused by cash-rich French clubs who were changing the entire rugby landscape, bosses at the region were refusing to be drawn into a battle with them.

A bracing walk along Aberavon seafront for players and residents of Sŵn y Môr care home in Port Talbot as part of the Ospreys' 'giving back to the community' programme

Instead, they were putting their faith in a successful, established development pathway which had ensured that the team already consisted of predominantly home grown, local talent, with more than 80 per cent of the squad hailing from within the region, the highest of all four regions.

An increase in their investment in development would, they believed, reap greater long-term rewards than spending big money attempting to match the telephone number salaries on offer in France.

Nevertheless, the 'galactico' tag had always been a tough one for the Ospreys to shrug off. The signs were, though, that this was starting to change.

Pre-season preparations began with an unfamiliar looking make-up to the squad, thanks to departures and international calls, but the mood was good.

As the new season approached, French side Lyon were the first opposition of the summer, romping to a comfortable 38–10 win in Switzerland, a result which would have done little to ease fan concerns despite the fact that on top of the absent internationals a number of additional players were left at home to spend more time working on conditioning.

A week later it was back to the Liberty Stadium as Russia became the second national team to take on the might of Ospreylia as they prepared for their RWC campaign, following the 2006 Wallabies, and they became the second to be defeated by the region, the Ospreys winning 46–19.

As August came to an end, 21-year-old Justin Tipuric was named as captain of the team for the opening weeks of the season in the absence of Alun Wyn Jones who was away at the World Cup, and the young open-side was to lead his home region into action with a ringing endorsement from Scott Johnson, who said: "Tips is a very mature, intelligent kid who is passionate about his home region. He may be quiet but he's a natural leader."

It was difficult to gauge where the team were after such contrasting warm-up games, but just days later the new season was upon the Ospreys, with a home game against Leinster to kick-off the new campaign, in the renamed RaboDirect PRO12.

Although both sides had an unfamiliar look about them due to the tournament just about to begin on the other side of the world, a tough evening was expected at the Liberty Stadium for the young Ospreys team.

However, they got the new campaign off to a flying start, a Rhys Webb try inside 100 seconds giving them a lead over the Irish side that they would never surrender, eventually winning 27–3, with further tries coming from Hanno Dirksen and Tipuric.

Buoyed by that stunning win, the Ospreys welcomed Edinburgh to Swansea the following weekend, and although they had to fight harder for the win, Tipuric's injury-time touchdown secured a 26–19 win to make it two from two.

Victory on the road over Benetton Treviso (32–27) in the sweltering late summer Italian heat was then followed by back-to-back home games once again. First up was a convincing 32–14 win against Ulster, and then a tough 26–21 success versus Connacht.

It had been an incredible opening month to the season, with five wins from five games before September was even out putting the Ospreys at the top of the formative PRO12 table.

Such had been the impression made on the watching rugby public by the young Ospreys that former skipper Barry Williams, the first ever centurion at the region and the first captain to lift silverware with the Ospreys, was moved to pay tribute to the team, describing them as 'a team with a cause'.

Speaking during the unbeaten start to the season, he added:

> If you try to play attractive rugby, with a young team who are local boys, the community will respond and get behind the team. I hope that the team can continue to grow and don't play with a fear of failing... If anyone says 'the Ospreys don't have any stars anymore' the simple answer is to take a look at the youth system, the money being spent there and the number of players coming through. That will be of more long-term benefit to rugby in the region than spending huge money on someone who doesn't believe in what the Ospreys are trying to do.

Round six saw the Ospreys back on the road, and the always tough test of facing Munster at Thomond

Park. It was a test that they passed with flying colours, despite going behind to a Danny Barnes try in only the second minute. The Irish led for an hour, but with the boot of Dan Biggar keeping the Ospreys in touch, a late Rhys Webb try ensured the unbeaten record remained intact as the league went into a two-week sabbatical.

Out in New Zealand, Wales had exceeded expectation and had reached the last four of the RWC, where they were narrowly beaten by France following an early red card for captain Sam Warburton, leaving them to play-off with Australia for third place.

Meanwhile, back home attention turned to the development LV= Cup competition, and the same evening as Welsh hearts had been broken at Eden Park, an Ospreys team featuring two debutants and five first starts in the XV and another potential five debutants on the bench unsurprisingly came unstuck on the road at Exeter.

A week later, with the Ospreys still missing their entire RWC contingent, Northampton Saints arrived in Bridgend to face the Ospreys in the LV= with a full-strength line-up as they looked to welcome back their England players from their own World Cup experience ahead of tougher games to come.

Despite the visitors being expected to romp to a comfortable win, a gallant showing from the inexperienced Ospreys ensured the Saints didn't have it all their own way, putting in a plucky performance in a 32–22 defeat to the side with vastly more experience.

Having lost their third place play-off to Australia by three points, the Wales squad headed home, but the Ospreys were still without them as they returned to league action, suffering a first defeat of the season away to Glasgow.

Rhys Webb gets the season off to a flying start with a try inside two minutes as the Ospreys thump Leinster on the opening day of the new season

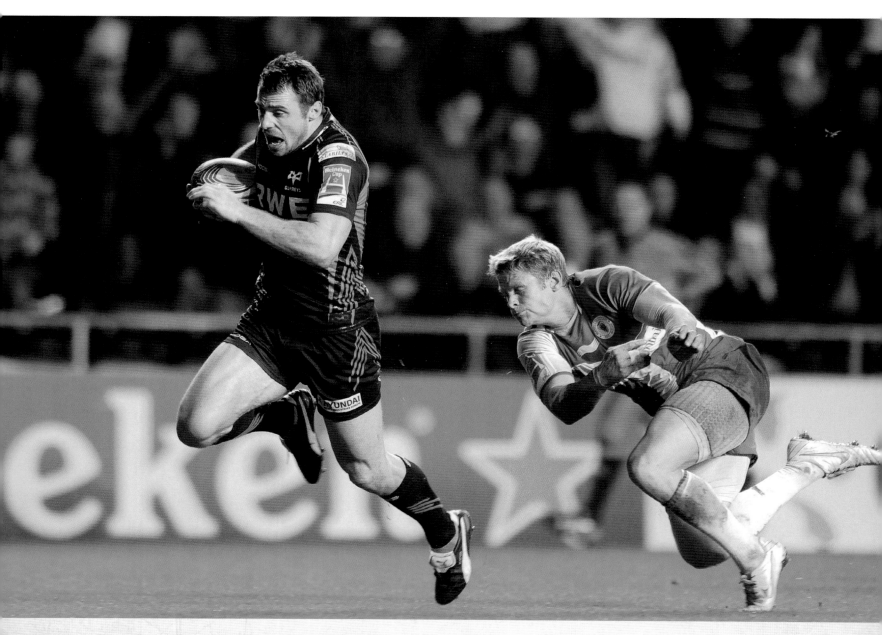

Iain Balshaw of Biarritz can't catch Tommy Bowe as he races through to score for the Ospreys

The following weekend saw the first derby match of the season, with the Scarlets visiting the Liberty, a game that coincided with the return of the Wales players, five of them stepping straight back into regional action.

However, despite being played on Bonfire Night, the eagerly awaited clash proved to be something of a damp squib, finishing all square at 9–9 as the returning World Cup players in both teams failed to fire.

There was little time to settle everyone back into the swing of things as the busy schedule saw the first weekend of the Heineken Cup just seven days later.

The Ospreys early season form had become a distant memory thanks to some stuttering work in recent weeks, albeit two of their three defeats in the last four games coming in the LV= Cup, but with the arrival of French giants Biarritz in Ospreylia, there was plenty to focus the mind.

It proved to be a memorable afternoon as Dan Biggar kicked 23 points to add to Tommy Bowe's try, giving the Ospreys a flying start in European competition, winning 28–21. A 26-all draw in Italy a week later against Treviso, albeit thanks to a last-minute kick from Matthew Morgan to level things, meant that the Ospreys were well in contention in their pool ahead of December's double-header against English champions Saracens.

In the meantime it was back to the PRO12 and an attempt to make up for the little stutter over the two previous rounds, and victories over Connacht on the road and at home to Munster kept the title challenge firmly on the road.

The Munster win, in particular, was pleasing for the coaching team coming as it did minus 19 players through international call-ups and injury, with the WRU organising an additional post-Rugby World Cup game against Australia for the same day.

Next up it was back to the Heineken Cup, and the two games that it was felt would shape the final outcome of pool five. Saracens came out on top over two tight matches played on back-to-back weekends.

First they claimed a 31–26 win at Wembley Stadium, despite two Ashley Beck tries, and then the following weekend they won 16–13 at the Liberty to inflict a first home defeat on the Ospreys in Europe for six years and 18 matches, to leave their hopes of progressing seemingly in tatters.

The four regions, under the Regional Rugby Wales banner, then announced the implementation of a £3.5m salary cap that would be brought in for the following season and would limit each organisation's salary expenditure – a sign that all four were having to face up to changing economic conditions.

A positive festive period with three Welsh derbies was needed to lift spirits at the Liberty Stadium, but instead, defeats on the road to the Scarlets (a first loss in the derby fixture in four years) and the Dragons sandwiched a home win over the Blues.

In the middle of all the on-the-pitch activity came the announcement hours after the Scarlets game on Boxing Day that Director of Coaching Scott Johnson was to stand down at the end of the season when his contract expired, to take up an offer to work with the Scottish Rugby Union.

Against that backdrop the Ospreys resumed their European campaign, making light work of Treviso in

The look says it all as the Ospreys scrape a draw in Treviso thanks to a last-minute Matthew Morgan penalty

Ashley Beck races through to score one of his two tries at Wembley against Saracens

a bonus-point win at the Liberty which meant they travelled to the south of France to face Biarritz, hoping to end on a high with a chance of securing a place in the Amlin Cup last eight, only to be blown away 38–5 in a match where they never got any kind of foothold.

With Europe over for another year and the Six Nations looming, it was LV= Cup time again, with a development side defeating Welsh rivals the Dragons in Bridgend before losing to Worcester in extreme wintry weather conditions.

Having begun the season so strongly, the campaign was in danger of sliding off the tracks as it moved into February, so a 15–14 win in Edinburgh in the next PRO12 fixture was a welcome boost after a disappointing run of results in all competitions, keeping the Ospreys in second place.

The match-winning score was a moment of individual magic from wing Hanno Dirksen which secured a second consecutive try of the year gong for the region at the PRO12 end of season awards.

Despite the disappointing exit from Europe and the Christmas PRO12 slump, the win in Scotland had moved the team back into second place, so if they could regain the consistency shown at the start of the season, a third consecutive play-off spot remained a likely possibility.

However, just days later, as the team prepared to face Aironi there was a day of unprecedented drama at the Liberty.

Members of the press were scheduled to arrive at midday on Wednesday, 15th February, for the weekly briefing ahead of the game, but before they arrived came a press release announcing the departure of Head Coach, Sean Holley after nine years.

Before the impact of that announcement had hit home came a second one, this time confirming that Director of Coaching, Scott Johnson, was also to leave with immediate effect rather than at the end of the season as had been previously announced.

As the press assembled at the home of the Ospreys, the question on everybody lips was who is going to replace the outgoing pair? They didn't have to wait long for an answer, as the doors to the media room were pushed open shortly after midday by Andrew Hore, accompanied by the new Head Coach, Ospreys' original, Steve Tandy.

Thirty-two-year-old Tandy was something of a surprise appointment to the eyes of the outside world, but one who had the respect of everybody within the Ospreys camp.

A gritty, hard-working back row in his playing days, he had made 102 regional appearances after previously playing for Neath. Displaying the same characteristics as a coach, he had cut his teeth on the Ospreys development pathway, first in age-grade regional rugby then as Head Coach at Bridgend, combined with the position of Technical Coach with the Ospreys.

He had particularly impressed management at the region when stepping up as acting Head Coach during the LV= Cup campaign, including the recent games against the Dragons and Worcester.

Hailing from within the region, Tandy was well aware of the pressures involved with the job: "Clearly there's an air of expectation on whoever is in charge at the Ospreys but having been here since the very beginning I know what to expect," he said.

Tandy was to be accompanied by Forwards Coach, Jonathan Humphreys, with a new Backs Coach to come

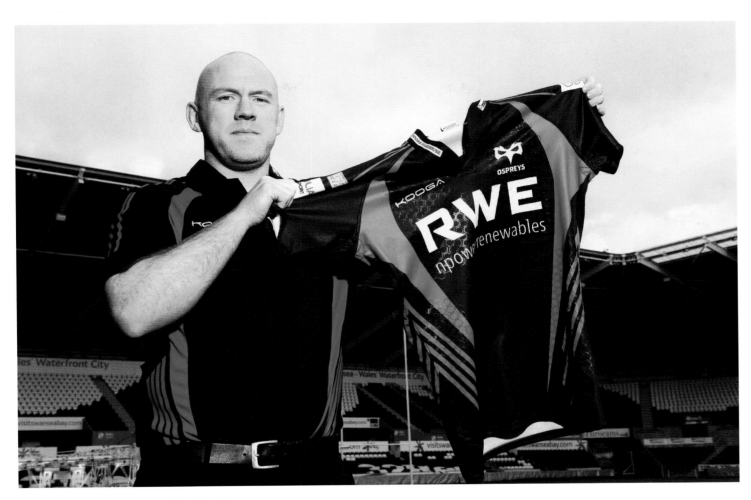

Steve Tandy takes the reins as Head Coach

in and complete the team, but there was no time to settle with the small matter of Aironi in just 48 hours time.

Tandy got the winning start he would have wanted, a scrappy 23–7 success, but that was followed by defeats in Ulster and at home to Glasgow, which left supporters looking down the table rather than up it as they feared for the Ospreys place in the play-off spots with just five games to go.

The Ospreys were boosted for that all-important run-in with the confirmation that Gruff Rees was returning to the region as Backs Coach less than nine months after joining Aironi, the former national Sevens and age-grade coach getting stuck straight in to the task of helping the Ospreys towards the play-offs.

With the region's ever sizable international contingent arriving back at Llandarcy at the end of March on the back of a third Six Nations Grand Slam in seven years, the expectation was on the senior professionals to provide the impetus to carry a young group over the finishing line. However, not even the most optimistic of Ospreys fans could have predicted what was to come over the final two months of the season.

First up was a trip to Leinster where the Ospreys overturned a 13-point second-half deficit despite being a man down, a late try from Richard Hibbard allowing Dan Biggar to secure a one-point win with a touchline conversion. Next, Treviso were seen off in style at the Liberty, a bonus-point win keeping the team in the top four.

A convincing 33–12 win over Cardiff Blues, that saw the Ospreys score 27 unanswered second-half points, moved them up into second place before the visit to the Liberty of the Dragons at the end of April.

It was an emotional evening for everyone in a bumper crowd of almost 15,000, for what was being billed as 'Shane's farewell'. Shane Williams, the region's all-time top try scorer, had already bowed out from international rugby at the end of 2012 and had now confirmed that he was hanging up his boots once the current season finished.

Fans flocked to the Liberty Stadium to pay tribute to him and the Ospreys responded in style with a bonus-point win. In typical

Hanno Dirksen scores as the Ospreys book a place in the PRO12 final with a stunning win over Munster at the Liberty Stadium

Shane style, he had the final say, scoring a try with the last play of the match, before converting his own score.

That win secured a home semi-final for the Ospreys in the play-offs with one round of fixtures still to play. After the final weekend, which saw the Ospreys win in Italy over Aironi, it was confirmed that Munster would be the opponents for what was anticipated would be a night of high drama at the Liberty.

In the end there was very little by way of drama as the hosts put on one of their greatest ever displays to totally overwhelm their opponents.

From start to finish it was one-way traffic as Munster failed to cope with the Ospreys who ran in five tries on the way to a record victory over the Irish giants, 45–10. Dan Biggar scored 22, including the first try, while Kahn Fotuali'i, Hanno Dirksen, Andrew Bishop and Rhys Webb also touched down.

Leinster's win over Glasgow in the other semi-final meant it was Leinster v Ospreys at the RDS in the final, for the second time in the three years of play-off rugby in the league.

Ospreys supporters were praying that lightning could strike twice after their 2010 final win in Dublin, but Leinster served a warning the week before the big match, securing their second consecutive Heineken Cup crown with a demolition job on Ulster.

More than 1,200 schoolchildren turned out to see the Ospreys off from the Liberty Stadium, watching their final training session in a show of support that was appreciated by everybody at the Ospreys before they set off for Dublin.

A long season that had begun with supporters doubting the future direction of their team and had seen ups and downs and coaching departures, was drawing to an exciting climax, with everything depending on the final 80 minutes, the last 80 minutes of Shane Williams' top-class career. Did the wing wizard have one more trick up his sleeve?

On a scorching hot afternoon in Dublin, a game of high drama ebbed and flowed as two teams at the peak of their game went head-to-head. Early on it was cagey stuff as Biggar and Jonathan Sexton traded penalties, before Leinster seized the initiative when Sean Cronin grabbed the first try of the afternoon 26 minutes in. An Isa Nacewa try stretched Leinster's lead, and although the boot of Biggar kept the Ospreys within touching distance they trailed by eight points at the break, 17–9.

The Ospreys needed a positive start to the second half and they got it through an Ashley Beck try, only for Sexton to nudge Leinster further ahead. Just short of the hour, up popped Shane to wriggle over in the corner for an unconverted score confirmed by the Television Match Official, bringing the team to within two points at 23–21 with a quarter of the game remaining.

Nacewa's second try, converted by Sexton, meant the Ospreys trailed by nine points, and as the game moved into the final six minutes, the win was looking increasingly unlikely.

However, another Biggar penalty meant a converted try would do it, and then, with just two minutes on

Shane Williams scores a last-minute try at the RDS to leave the Ospreys trailing by a point with the conversion to come...

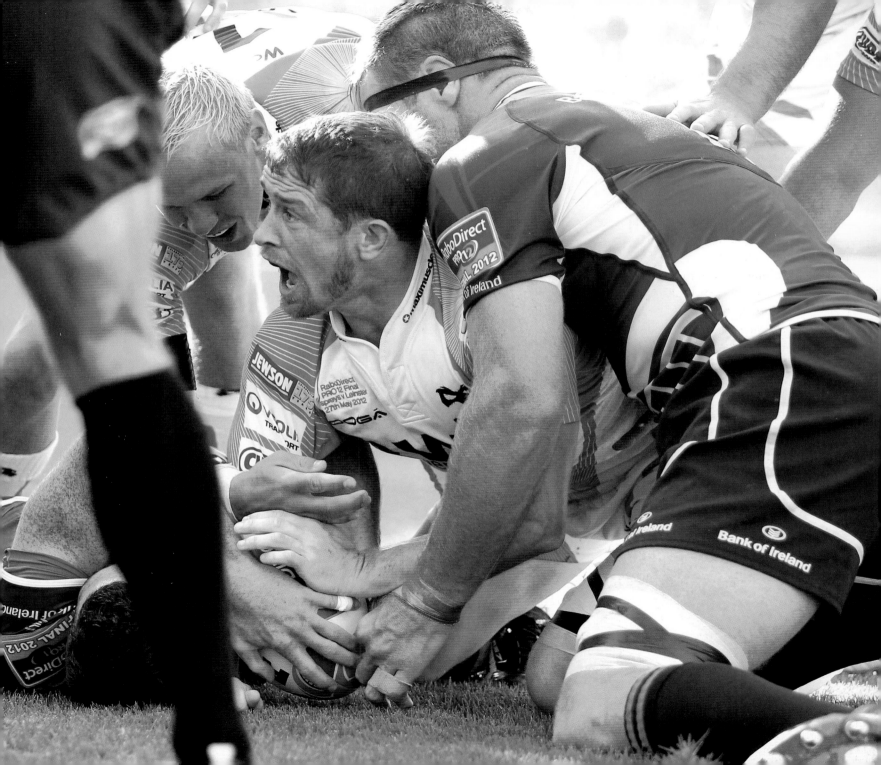

The pressure is on but Dan Biggar nails the conversion to wrestle the PRO12 title out of Leinster's grasp

Champions again

the clock, Shane once again crossed in the corner for a second try, again confirmed by the TMO, to unbelievably leave Biggar kicking for the match with just seconds remaining.

He showed nerves of steel to slot over the pressure kick from the touchline to secure an incredible win for the Ospreys, a record fourth Celtic League title, and the second time they had mugged Leinster in their own back yard.

Amidst scenes of wild celebration, Steve Tandy hailed the 'fantastic' Ospreys, saying: "They have been fantastic since I took over and were relentless today. It's

been a turbulent season but we've earned this title. It's an exciting time for us, with young talent and a wealth of experience. It's a good combination."

The final word on a memorable afternoon, a memorable season, and for that matter, a memorable career, goes to try-scoring hero Shane Williams, who said after the final whistle:

We've worked very hard this season, we've had our ups and downs, there's been change in the ranks, and for us to stick at it as we have, the guys are to be commended. I'll never forget this day... For us to stick at it and play right to the 80th minute, and we had to play right to

The celebrations continue behind closed doors at the RDS

Captain and coach enjoy a moment together to savour the success

the 80th minute, shows what we are about. It wasn't our best performance of the season by a long shot but it was commendable in the way we played right to the end... We've got a squad that's good enough to come to the RDS for a final and beat probably one of the best teams there's ever been. We've got strength in depth in this squad now, we've got a lot of young talent coming through and there are champions in this squad who are still in their first season. These boys are the future now and it's time for me to take a back seat and let them drive the Ospreys forward.

10

With a fourth league title safely tucked away in the Liberty Stadium trophy cabinet, there was certainly a more positive vibe about the place than a year previously.

A record number of more than 8,000 season tickets had already been shifted by the end of May, such an exciting end of season really firing the public's imagination.

It wasn't all champagne and roses in Ospreylia though. A HMRC High Court petition that had come to light the day after the play-off win in Dublin was still hanging over the business, while the salary cap had meant that once again a number of players had departed over the summer.

Although Shane Williams and Paul James were the only players from the 23 that faced Leinster at the end of May heading through the exit door, other big names were also leaving, including wingers Tommy Bowe and Nikki Walker. Along with centre Sonny Parker, another departee, it meant that the Ospreys were losing their four top all-time try scorers who between them had touched down an incredible 159 times on regional duty.

The only inward movement saw centre Jonathan Spratt returning after a year at London Irish, while Tom Smith did a U-turn on his own decision to move to Irish and opted to stay at the Liberty.

Nevertheless, with youngsters such as Hanno Dirksen and Eli Walker coming through on the wing, along with the likes of Ashley Beck, Justin Tipuric, James King and Ryan Bevington also starting to shine, there was a genuine belief that this hard-working, young and predominantly local group could build on the fantastic climax to the previous year.

The return to training after the summer lay-off, as always, was very much a staggered one with the region's senior and U20 international contingent arriving back to work later than the core group of players.

There was a huge off-the-field boost as July drew to a close, with confirmation that the dispute with HMRC had been resolved, allowing the board to continue their behind the scenes work to put the business on a sounder financial footing without the shadow of the taxman hanging over them.

Preparations for the new campaign began in earnest at the start of August as the team headed across to France for a week-long training camp in the Puy de Dôme area, culminating in a game against T14 giants Clermont Auvergne, a team packed with some of world rugby's biggest names. By contrast, the Ospreys would be fielding a team minus any of its international contingent.

More than 2,000 fans turned up for the unveiling of the 2012/13 kit at Swansea's National Waterfront Museum

As such, it came as no surprise to see the French side securing what was, in the end, a comfortable 49–25 win, the perfect build-up for their league opener just a week later. For the Ospreys though, it was a valuable step-up in their pre-season preparations, with a home game to follow against Bath in eight days' time.

Before then though there was the small matter of the launch of the new jersey for the coming season. The Ospreys jersey had consistently proven to be the

The heat of battle as the Ospreys secure their first win of the season at Parc y Scarlets

second biggest seller in the UK and Ireland, and more than 2,000 fans turned out at the National Waterfront Museum in Swansea for their first glimpse of the shirt – which this year featured the names of every one of the region's 77 community rugby clubs – with the highest opening weekend sales of any Ospreys jersey ever.

With the news that season ticket sales were now passed 9,000, double the previous year and providing a revenue increase of almost 50 per cent year on year, defeat to Bath at the Liberty failed to quash the feel-good factor off the field.

The opening weekend of the season fast approaching, Tandy was questioned by the Welsh

Dan Biggar, Jonathan Spratt and Tom Grabham get stuck in at Glynneath Training Centre as the Ospreys take part in Neath Port Talbot Council for Voluntary Services' annual Volunteers' Day

media on how he felt his squad would cope given the departures since the end of the previous campaign.

Although bullish about his team's chances, the Ospreys 'original' also sounded a word of caution that would, in nine months or so and with the benefit of hindsight, be painfully accurate:

We've lost players and that's something we've got to deal with… We know what it is, we've got a budget to work to. We've got to go and find the next Shane, the next Tommy Bowe. We can't dwell on it; we've just got to move on. Yes, in certain areas we are thin. But, it's our job as coaches to go and find the next generation… Obviously you could have a couple of injuries in

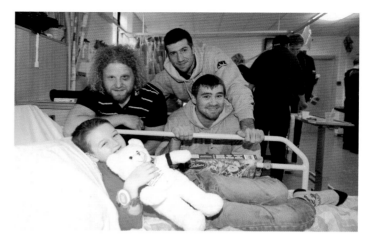

Ospreys players at the Children's Ward at Morriston Hospital for their regular Christmas visit

certain departments which may leave you looking a bit threadbare, but a lot of squads out there are the same. You could be lucky or unlucky with injury.

However, the upbeat mood in the camp was swept away in the opening weeks of the campaign. Three straight defeats, two at home, was not the start that the defending champions had hoped for.

A first ever defeat against Italian opposition on the opening day of the season, away to Treviso, was followed by back-to-back losses at home against Ulster and then Glasgow which left the Ospreys in a position which nobody would have predicted just a few weeks ago, with just two losing bonus points to their credit and already having to play catch-up on their rivals.

The Ospreys were already in danger of losing their grip on the title before the first month was up but if there's ever a game to focus the minds of any Ospreylian, then it's a West Wales derby against the Scarlets and that's what was next up for the region, away at Parc y Scarlets.

By contrast, the old enemy had started the season in fine form with a 100 per cent record and were sitting on top of the early season PRO12 table. The pundits were predicting an easy win for the hosts, mystified with the poor start to the season from the Ospreys.

Skipper Alun Wyn Jones seemed to hit the nail on the head pre-match when he said: "They will be baying for blood from the west and you can't blame them – it's a derby."

The capacity crowd was on the edge of their seats throughout a robust encounter, and with just ten minutes left it was tied at 9–9. However, the Ospreys' greater physicality eventually wore down their opposition, late tries from Ryan Jones and Hanno Dirksen securing a first win of the season, despite a late score for the Scarlets from George North.

Joe Bearman soars high to collect the ball at Rodney Parade

It was an impressive, and crucial, win but had it stopped the rot or was it just a temporary respite? One thing was for sure; there was little margin for error over the coming weeks if the Ospreys were going to stay in the hunt.

Munster were seen off in some style at the Liberty Stadium the following weekend before a bonus-point win in Italy over Zebre meant that the table was looking a lot healthier as the focus turned to the Heineken Cup.

Arguably the biggest news of the month, though, came in between those two games. Amidst the continuing behind the scenes machinations to get the business onto a more secure footing, Managing Director Mike Cuddy, who had played such an influential role alongside Roger Blyth to establish the Ospreys in

Travelling Ospreys fans get behind their team despite a defeat in Toulouse

its formative years, was to relinquish his post with immediate effect, although he would remain on the board as a director.

The European campaign began with a bonus-point win against Treviso at the Liberty before the Ospreys were unfortunate to leave Welford Road in Leicester empty-handed after the Tigers scored three tries in the last eight minutes to somehow turn a closely

fought contest into a 17-point win, leaving what Tandy described as "a very disappointed dressing room".

Back in the PRO12, the winning run continued with home wins over Connacht and Leinster, while the announcement of the national squad for the autumn international series once again saw the region again lead the way with ten players, including first-time call-up Aaron Jarvis.

However, pride at such a large representation was tempered considerably over the course of November as injury struck a number of players on national duty. Jarvis, Dan Biggar, Ian Evans, Richard Hibbard, Adam Jones and Alun Wyn Jones were all sent back to the region with injuries of varying degrees, while the likes of Hanno Dirksen, Tom Smith and Joe Rees were all ruled out for the season by the Ospreys' own medical staff, leaving the smaller squad looking very stretched.

Youthful Ospreys teams took to the field in the LV= Cup, with a win and defeat to show for their efforts against Gloucester and Exeter, before defeat to Edinburgh and a home win over Cardiff, both in the PRO12, at the end of the month.

Next up was a trip to Stade Ernest-Wallon to face Toulouse in the Heineken Cup. Always a daunting challenge at the best of times, an appalling injury list, including all three Heineken Cup registered tight heads, made it even more so on this occasion.

Front row cover arrived in the shape of former All Black Campbell Johnstone, now playing in Spain of all places, untried Moldovan international Dmitri Arhip, and former Osprey Cai Griffiths on loan from London Irish, having only left the Liberty in the summer after making over 100 appearances for the region.

As if the injury list hadn't upset preparations enough, the team then suffered an eight-hour delay in departures at Bristol Airport the day before the game, making what most observers had already declared an impossible job even harder.

A youthful team with seven Heineken Cup debutants, in truth, never stood much chance at the home of the four-time winners, but the way they went about the task in a 30–14 defeat made many people sit up and take notice, and led skipper for the day, Kahn Fotuali'i, to declare: "I'm very, very proud of the effort. It says something about the future of Ospreys Rugby. There are young boys coming through, the future is looking bright if they keep their mind on the job and strive to wear an Ospreylian jersey. It's really looking positive."

Unbelievably, with just a seven-day turnaround, the Ospreys were able to reverse that score-line in the return fixture and secure possibly their best ever win in European competition. A try for one of the youngsters making a big impression, Eli Walker, helped the Ospreys to a memorable 17–6 win.

It was back to domestic duty over Christmas and wins over the Scarlets (32–3) and the Dragons (14–3), before a tight victory over Zebre took the Ospreys into the PRO12 top four for the first time.

Leicester were next, in a do-or-die European tie at the Liberty. A win was essential if there was to be any hope of progressing to the quarters, and the region led by a converted try going into the final quarter. However, on an afternoon of drama and tension a late try from Jonathan Spratt could only secure a share of the spoils against the English champions at 15-all, the usually reliable Dan Biggar missing three early kicks that would have made such a big difference.

Defeats over the next three weeks, to Treviso, Dragons and Harlequins ended Ospreys involvement in the two knockout competitions, leaving them to focus on their PRO12 defence.

The performance of the Ospreys youngsters hadn't

Just a week later, young wing Eli Walker scored to inspire a memorable win over the French giants

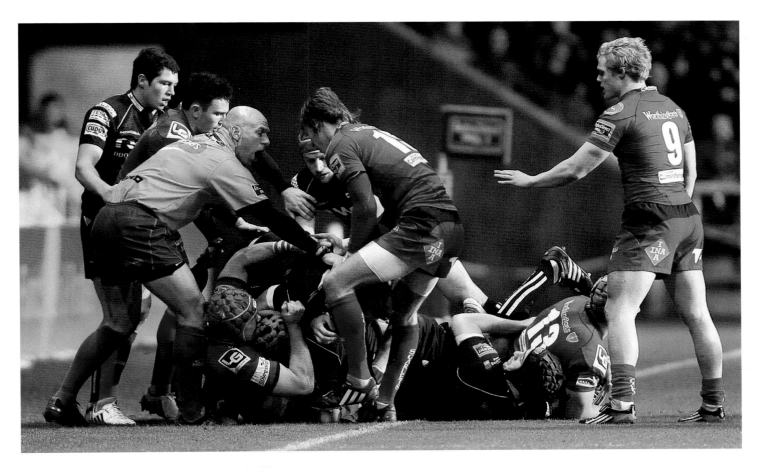

Tempers fray during the Boxing Day derby at the Liberty

gone unnoticed, with Sam Lewis and Morgan Allen nominated for breakthrough player awards by LV= and with James King and Eli Walker getting their first international call-ups among the regular sizeable Ospreys contingent in the Welsh squad.

With the Six Nations underway, the Ospreys faced the difficult task of travelling to big spending Ulster, unbeaten at home all season and top of the table with an experienced core of overseas players, missing 26 players through injury or international duty and with a line-up that again featured a number of debutants.

Despite the incredible team spirit that was being

Kahn Fotuali'i congratulates Ryan Bevington on his match-winning try in Ulster

James King runs in a crucial try against Cardiff Blues at the Millennium Stadium

displayed by a young group week-in, week-out, no-one anticipated an Ospreys win, but a performance described at the time by BBC *Scrum V* presenter Ross Harries as 'full of character' saw the odds upset once again as the visitors left Belfast with the points after a 16–12 win.

Injuries and international call-ups continued to hamper the Ospreys hopes, a win, a draw and a defeat in the next three games most notable for the backline sent out to face Edinburgh featuring four scrum halves, as the coaches came close to simply running out of players.

Buoyed by the return of their international players off the back of a successful Six Nations campaign where they had again won the Championship courtesy of a crushing win over England in the final game, the Ospreys responded with a record victory over the Dragons at the Liberty (52–19), running in seven tries to move into the play-off spots just ahead of the Scarlets with four games to go.

Over the next few days there was mixed news in the camp, first disappointment when in line with the bad luck that had run right through the season, impressive 20-year-old wing Eli Walker was ruled out of the closing weeks.

The good news saw Dan Biggar signing a new three-year deal with the region, bucking the trend of the season which had seen numerous big Welsh names confirm they were leaving Wales as the effects of the salary cap bit hard in the face of big money offers elsewhere.

Biggar's commitment to his home region shone through when he said: "This is an organisation that has always been very good to me and supported me so it's great that I can recognise that by committing my future to the region."

There was still plenty of work to be done if the Ospreys were to secure a play-off spot, and a win over the Blues at the Millennium

Tom Isaacs slides in to score a late try on the final day in Dublin, giving the Ospreys belated hope of a play-off place

End of season heartbreak as the final whistle goes in Dublin and the Ospreys fail to make the play-offs.

Stadium in the first ever Welsh regional double-header kept them in the driving seat.

While the play-off battle was ongoing, the Ospreys again highlighted how far the organisation was changing with the appointment of two new directors to the board, Tyrone Davies and Debra Williams, the first female to hold such a position in the Welsh game, confirmed as non-executive directors.

Treviso were seen off at the Liberty Stadium,

allowing the Ospreys to stay just ahead of the Scarlets with two games to go. However, although the Ospreys held fourth place on points' difference, they had the more difficult of the run-ins, with away games against teams in the top three, Glasgow and Leinster, while the Scarlets had, on paper, the easier games, finishing at home against the Blues and Treviso.

The Ospreys travelled to Scotland on the penultimate weekend with a team that was once more hamstrung by injury, eleven players missing. However, no-one was expecting what unfolded over 80 minutes in Glasgow as the hosts ran in five tries for a convincing victory over a tired-looking Ospreys team that, if truth be told, looked ready for the end of the season.

A Scarlets win over the Blues meant that they leapfrogged the Ospreys into fourth and looked odds on to secure the final play-off spot.

It was to go down to the wire, but in the lead-up to the regular season finale, came the sideshow of the British & Irish Lions squad announcement ahead of their tour to Australia.

Still the pinnacle of any player's career, as was the case in 2009, the Ospreys were proud to again have the highest number included of any of the four Welsh regions. Of the five Ospreys named, two were second-time Lions, Adam and Alun Wyn Jones, while Ian Evans, Richard Hibbard and Justin Tipuric were honoured by selection for the first time.

With the Lions selection out of the way, the focus returned to the PRO12 and a return to the scene of last season's incredible play-off final win, for a final-day clash with Leinster. This time, the Ospreys prepared for the game knowing that not even a repeat of that memorable day may have been enough as the Scarlets started the day four points clear thanks to results in the previous round.

A Scarlets win would be the end of the story, an unlikely loss at the hands of Treviso would mean that an Ospreys win would see them through. For their part, the Italians did an incredible job, securing a barely believable 41–17 win in West Wales.

The Ospreys, however, couldn't keep their end up.

Falling behind early on at the RDS, they trailed by 14 points barely a quarter of the way through the game. A strong rally saw Dan Biggar and Ben John touching down and they trailed by just five at the break, but Leinster had too much in the second half, Tom Isaacs' late try coming in vain as the hosts won 37–19.

It had been a valiant effort in adversity by the Ospreys, 80 minutes that had pretty much summed up their season. There had been plenty of promise as unknown youngsters made their mark, but ultimately, a series of injuries had stripped the squad of too much experience and quality for them to truly thrive.

As Tandy had prophetically suggested back in August, with such a thin squad the Ospreys were reliant on staying relatively injury free if they were to successfully defend their crown. The reality had turned out to be something different.

Reflecting on the tenth season of the Ospreys though, Tandy refused to be downbeat, highlighting that the unexpected experience gained by youngsters thrust into frontline action over the course of the season would stand them in good stead:

> If you look back to last year, at the end of the season there was a huge turnover of players here but I think we've settled as a group over the course of the last twelve months… We've learnt a lot more about the group and we've got young players who have experienced Heineken Cup rugby and not looked out of place. We're in a pretty exciting place, we really are, and the future looks very bright.

One thing is for sure. If the first ten years of the Ospreys is anything to go by, the future would be nothing if not eventful…

2003—04 Seasons Results & Player Stats

Date	Team 1			Team 2	Venue	
15/08/03	Narberth	0	42	Ospreys	Lewis Lloyd Ground	
22/08/03	Ospreys	33	19	Worcester Warriors	The Gnoll	
05/09/03	Ospreys	41	30	Ulster	The Gnoll	Tries: Gavin Henson (2), Adrian Durston, Dave Tiueti; Cons: Shaun Connor (2), Gavin Henson; Pens: Shaun Connor (4), Gavin Henson
12/09/03	Newport Gwent Dragons	29	19	Ospreys	Rodney Parade	Tries: James Storey; Cons: Gavin Henson; Pens: Gavin Henson (4)
19/09/03	Leinster	35	21	Ospreys	Donnybrook	Tries: Elvis Seveali'I, Gavin Henson; Cons: Gavin Henson; Pens: Gavin Henson (3)
27/09/03	Ospreys	33	26	Munster	St Helen's	Tries: Andy Williams, Dave Tiueti, James Storey; Cons: Gavin Henson (3); Pens: Gavin Henson (4)
11/10/03	Celtic Warriors	22	32	Ospreys	Riverside Hardware Brewery Field	Tries: Gareth Morris (2; Cons: Gavin Henson (2; Pens: Gavin Henson (6)
17/10/03	Ospreys	42	18	Edinburgh Rugby	The Gnoll	Tries: Andrew Newman, James Storey, Scott Gibbs, Shaun Connor; Cons: Gavin Henson (2; Pens: Gavin Henson (6)
25/10/03	Cardiff Blues	43	6	Ospreys	Cardiff Arms Park	Pens: Gavin Henson (2)
31/10/03	Ospreys	22	33	Connacht	St Helen's	Tries: Chris Wells; Cons: Shaun Connor; Pens: Shaun Connor (4), Adrian Durston
07/11/03	Border Reivers	22	16	Ospreys	Netherdale Stadium	Tries: Gavin Thomas; Cons: Gavin Henson; Pens: Gavin Henson (2); DG: Shaun Connor
29/11/03	Ospreys	25	36	Leinster	The Gnoll	Tries: Huw Bennett; Cons: Gavin Henson; Pens: Gavin Henson (5); DG: Shaun Connor
07/12/03	Leeds Carnegie	29	20	Ospreys	Headingley Carnegie	Tries: Scott Gibbs, Shane Williams; Cons: Shaun Connor (2); Pens: Shaun Connor; DG: Shaun Connor
12/12/03	Ospreys	16	32	Edinburgh Rugby	St Helen's	Tries: Dave Tiueti, Scott Gibbs; Pens: Shaun Connor (2)
02/01/04	Scarlets	28	15	Ospreys	Stradey Park	Pens: Shaun Connor (5)
10/01/04	Stade Toulousain	29	6	Ospreys	Stade Ernest-Wallon	Pens: Gavin Henson (2)
16/01/04	Ospreys	11	29	Stade Toulousain	The Gnoll	Tries: Gavin Henson; Pens: Gavin Henson (2)
23/01/04	Edinburgh Rugby	33	15	Ospreys	Meadowbank	Pens: Gavin Henson (5)
31/01/04	Ospreys	10	3	Leeds Carnegie	St Helen's	Tries: Andy Williams; Cons: Gavin Henson; Pens: Gavin Henson
06/02/04	Ospreys	33	11	Glasgow Warriors	The Gnoll	Tries: Dave Tiueti, Gavin Henson, Shaun Connor; Cons: Gavin Henson (3); Pens: Gavin Henson (4)
13/02/04	Ulster	31	19	Ospreys	Ravenhill	Tries: Barry Williams, Dave Tiueti, Gareth Morris; Cons: Gavin Henson, Shaun Connor
20/02/04	Ospreys	26	14	Newport Gwent Dragons	St Helen's	Tries: Nathan Bonner-Evans (2), Dave Tiueti; Cons: Gavin Henson; Pens: Gavin Henson (3)
27/02/04	Munster	15	18	Ospreys	Musgrave Park	Tries: Elvis Seveali'I (2); Cons: Shaun Connor; Pens: Shaun Connor, DG: Shaun Connor
05/03/04	Ospreys	23	11	Celtic Warriors	The Gnoll	Tries: James Bater, Stefan Terblanche; Cons: Shaun Connor (2); Pens: Shaun Connor (3)
12/03/04	Edinburgh Rugby	31	35	Ospreys	Meadowbank	Tries: Andrew Millward, James Storey, Richie Pugh, Stefan Terblanche; Cons: Gavin Henson (3); Pens: Gavin Henson (3)
28/03/04	Ospreys	34	13	Cardiff Blues	St Helen's	Tries: Andrew Newman, Gavin Henson, Shaun Connor; Cons: Gavin Henson (2); Pens: Gavin Henson (5)
03/04/04	Connacht	24	21	Ospreys	The Sportsground	Tries: James Bater, Steve Tandy; Cons: Gavin Henson; Pens: Gavin Henson (3)
16/04/04	Ospreys	60	7	Border Reivers	The Gnoll	Tries: Gavin Henson (3), Shane Williams (2), Andy Williams, Elvis Seveali'I, Jonathan Thomas, Stefan Terblanche; Cons: Gavin Henson (6); Pens: Gavin Henson
30/04/04	Leinster	16	16	Ospreys	Donnybrook	Tries: Shane Williams; Cons: Gavin Henson; Pens: Gavin Henson (3)
09/05/04	Ospreys	15	18	Scarlets	St Helen's	Tries: Shane Williams, Stefan Terblanche; Cons: Gavin Henson; Pens: Gavin Henson
14/05/04	Glasgow Warriors	34	31	Ospreys	Hughenden	Tries: Andrew Newman, Duncan Jones, Jonathan Thomas, Richie Pugh; Cons: Gavin Henson (4); Pens: Gavin Henson

Player	P	W	D	L	Pts	Try	Con	Pen	DG	YC	RC
Lyndon Bateman	7	4	0	3	0	0	0	0	0	1	0
James Bater	25	12	1	12	10	2	0	0	0	2	0
Huw Bennett	5	0	0	5	5	1	0	0	0	0	0
Nathan Bonner-Evans	27	10	1	16	10	2	0	0	0	0	0
Matthew Brayley	4	4	0	0	0	0	0	0	0	0	0
Andrew Clatworthy	3	2	0	1	0	0	0	0	0	0	0
Shaun Connor	26	11	1	14	105	3	9	20	4	0	0
Alun Wyn Davies	1	0	0	1	0	0	0	0	0	0	0
Adrian Durston	17	6	0	11	8	1	0	1	0	0	0
Tim Evans	4	3	0	1	0	0	0	0	0	0	0
Scott Gibbs	17	4	0	12	15	3	0	0	0	1	0
Cai Griffiths	8	4	0	4	0	0	0	0	0	0	0
Gavin Henson	26	12	1	13	318	9	36	67	0	0	0
Pat Horgan	1	0	0	1	0	0	0	0	0	0	0
Paul James	13	6	1	6	0	0	0	0	0	0	0
Adam Jones	13	4	1	8	0	0	0	0	0	0	0
Duncan Jones	10	3	1	6	5	1	0	0	0	1	0
Matt Jones	1	0	0	1	0	0	0	0	0	0	0
Paul Jones	2	0	0	2	0	0	0	0	0	0	0
Gareth Llewellyn	6	0	0	6	0	0	0	0	0	1	0
Andy Lloyd	10	7	0	3	0	0	0	0	0	0	0
Andrew Millward	28	12	0	16	5	1	0	0	0	2	0
Gareth Morris	12	5	0	7	15	3	0	0	0	0	0
Andrew Newman	29	12	1	16	15	3	0	0	0	1	0
Richie Pugh	17	7	1	9	10	2	0	0	0	0	0
Elvis Seveali'i	22	10	1	11	20	4	0	0	0	0	0
James Storey	21	8	1	12	20	4	0	0	0	2	0
Luke Tait	20	11	1	8	0	0	0	0	0	0	0
Steve Tandy	21	10	1	10	5	1	0	0	0	2	0
Stefan Terblanche	19	8	1	10	20	4	0	0	0	0	0
Gavin Thomas	15	4	0	11	5	1	0	0	0	1	0
Jonathan Thomas	12	2	1	9	10	2	0	0	0	0	0
Dave Tiueti	27	11	1	15	30	6	0	0	0	0	0
Chris Wells	10	5	0	5	5	1	0	0	0	1	0
Rhodri Wells	4	4	0	0	0	0	0	0	0	0	0
Andy Williams	29	12	1	16	15	3	0	0	0	1	0
Barry Williams	26	11	1	16	5	1	0	0	0	0	0
Shane Williams	13	2	1	10	25	5	0	0	0	0	0

2004—05 Seasons Results & Player Stats

Date	Team 1			Team 2	Venue	
12/08/04	Stade Toulousain	28	14	Ospreys	Bagnères	
26/08/04	Ospreys	5	15	Bath Rugby	St Helen's	
03/09/04	Ospreys	34	17	Munster	St Helen's	Tries: Adrian Durston, Dai Bishop, Jason Spice, Lyndon Bateman; Cons: Gavin Henson (4); Pens: Gavin Henson (2)
10/09/04	Scarlets	6	23	Ospreys	Stradey Park	Tries: Gavin Henson, Richie Pugh; Cons: Gavin Henson (2); Pens: Gavin Henson (3)
18/09/04	Ospreys	39	3	Cardiff Blues	The Gnoll	Tries: Dai Bishop, Duncan Jones, Gavin Henson, Jason Spice, Sonny Parker; Cons: Gavin Henson (4); Pens: Gavin Henson (2)
25/09/04	Ulster	24	37	Ospreys	Ravenhill	Tries: Dai Bishop, Dave Tiueti, Shane Williams, Sonny Parker; Cons: Gavin Henson (4); Pens: Gavin Henson (2); DG: Gavin Henson
02/10/04	Ospreys	40	17	Glasgow Warriors	The Gnoll	Tries: Andrew Millward, Dai Bishop, Richard Mustoe, Ryan Jones, Sonny Parker, Steve Tandy; Cons: Gavin Henson (2); Pens: Gavin Henson (2)
08/10/04	Border Reivers	15	23	Ospreys	Netherdale Stadium	Tries: Andrew Newman, Ryan Jones; Cons: Gavin Henson (2); Pens: Gavin Henson (3)
15/10/04	Ospreys	11	3	Leinster	St Helen's	Tries: Sonny Parker; Pens: Gavin Henson (2)
23/10/04	Castres Olympique	38	17	Ospreys	Stade Pierre-Antoine	Tries: Adam Jones, Jason Spice; Cons: Gavin Henson (2); Pens: Gavin Henson
31/10/04	Ospreys	18	20	Munster	The Gnoll	Pens: Gavin Henson (6)
05/11/04	Newport Gwent Dragons	33	29	Ospreys	Rodney Parade	Tries: Dave Tiueti, Jason Spice; Cons: Matt Jones (2); Pens: Matt Jones (5)
12/11/04	Edinburgh Rugby	15	31	Ospreys	Murrayfield	Tries: Aled Brew, Andrew Newman, Stefan Terblanche; Cons: Matt Jones (2); Pens: Matt Jones (2); DG: Matt Jones, Shaun Connor
21/11/04	Ospreys	9	10	Connacht	The Gnoll	Pens: Matt Jones (2); DG: Matt Jones
05/12/04	Ospreys	24	7	Harlequins	St Helen's	Pens: Gavin Henson (8)
11/12/04	Harlequins	19	46	Ospreys	Twickenham Stoop	Tries: Gavin Henson (2), Matt Jones, Ryan Jones, Shane Williams, Stefan Terblanche; Cons: Gavin Henson (5); Pens: Gavin Henson (2)
18/12/04	Munster	13	9	Ospreys	Musgrave Park	Pens: Gavin Henson (3)
26/12/04	Ospreys	28	7	Scarlets	The Gnoll	Tries: Shane Williams (2), Barry Williams, James Bater; Cons: Matt Jones; Pens: Gavin Henson (2)
01/01/05	Cardiff Blues	9	15	Ospreys	Cardiff Arms Park	Tries: Jason Spice, Richie Pugh; Cons: Gavin Henson; Pens: Gavin Henson
08/01/05	Munster	20	10	Ospreys	Thomond Park	Tries: Shane Williams; Cons: Gavin Henson; Pens: Gavin Henson
15/01/05	Ospreys	20	11	Castres Olympique	The Gnoll	Tries: Elvis Seveali'I, Richie Rees; Cons: Gavin Henson (2); Pens: Gavin Henson (2)
21/01/05	Ospreys	22	21	Ulster	St Helen's	Tries: Gavin Henson; Cons: Gavin Henson; Pens: Gavin Henson (5)
29/01/05	Glasgow Warriors	27	27	Ospreys	Hughenden	Tries: Andrew Millward, Richie Rees, Stefan Terblanche; Cons: Matt Jones (2), Shaun Connor; Pens: Shaun Connor (2)
19/02/05	Ospreys	34	10	Border Reivers	The Gnoll	Tries: Andrew Millward, Andrew Newman, James Bater, Richie Pugh; Cons: Shaun Connor (4); Pens: Shaun Connor (2)
06/03/05	Leinster	12	16	Ospreys	Lansdowne Road	Tries: Jason Spice; Cons: Matt Jones; Pens: Shaun Connor (2), Matt Jones
18/03/05	Ospreys	30	0	Newport Gwent Dragons	St Helen's	Tries: Jason Spice (2), Adrian Durston, Richard Mustoe; Cons: Shaun Connor (2); Pens: Shaun Connor (2)
26/03/05	Ospreys	29	12	Edinburgh Rugby	The Gnoll	Tries: Gavin Henson, Jason Spice; Cons: Gavin Henson (2); Pens: Gavin Henson (5)
10/04/05	Connacht	13	22	Ospreys	The Sportsground	Tries: Gavin Henson, Jonathan Thomas, Shane Williams; Cons: Gavin Henson (2); Pens: Gavin Henson
30/04/05	Ospreys	23	16	Ulster	St Helen's	Tries: Matt Jones, Stefan Terblanche; Cons: Matt Jones (2); Pens: Matt Jones (3)
07/05/05	Scarlets	23	15	Ospreys	Stradey Park	Pens: Matt Jones (5)

Player	P	W	D	L	Pts	Try	Con	Pen	DG	YC	RC
Lyndon Bateman	18	14	1	3	5	1	0	0	0	1	0
James Bater	23	15	1	7	10	2	0	0	0	0	0
Lee Beach	1	1	0	0	0	0	0	0	0	0	0
Huw Bennett	4	3	0	1	0	0	0	0	0	0	0
Andrew Bishop	5	4	0	1	0	0	0	0	0	0	0
Dai Bishop	21	15	1	5	20	4	0	0	0	0	0
Nathan Bonner-Evans	7	4	1	2	0	0	0	0	0	0	0
Aled Brew	4	2	0	2	5	1	0	0	0	0	0
Brent Cockbain	16	11	0	5	0	0	0	0	0	2	0
Shaun Connor	6	5	1	0	41	0	7	8	1	0	0
Mefin Davies	5	4	0	1	0	0	0	0	0	0	0
Adrian Durston	25	18	1	6	10	2	0	0	0	0	0
Cai Griffiths	3	3	0	0	0	0	0	0	0	0	0
Gavin Henson	19	15	0	4	265	7	34	53	1	0	0
Richard Hibbard	10	8	0	2	0	0	0	0	0	0	0
James Hook	1	1	0	0	0	0	0	0	0	0	0
Paul James	21	14	1	6	0	0	0	0	0	0	0
Adam Jones	17	12	0	5	5	1	0	0	0	0	0
Duncan Jones	20	16	0	4	5	1	0	0	0	1	0
Matt Jones	23	16	1	6	90	2	10	18	2	0	0
Ryan Jones	20	16	0	4	15	3	0	0	0	1	1
Andy Lloyd	17	12	1	4	0	0	0	0	0	0	0
Paul Mackey	1	0	1	0	0	0	0	0	0	0	0
Andrew Millward	24	17	1	6	15	3	0	0	0	2	0
Richard Mustoe	14	10	0	4	10	2	0	0	0	1	0
Andrew Newman	25	17	1	7	15	3	0	0	0	0	0
Sonny Parker	17	13	0	4	20	4	0	0	0	0	0
Richie Pugh	26	19	0	7	15	3	0	0	0	0	0
Richie Rees	7	6	1	0	10	2	0	0	0	1	0
Elvis Seveali'i	20	13	1	6	5	1	0	0	0	1	0
Jason Spice	26	18	1	7	45	9	0	0	0	2	0
Luke Tait	6	5	0	1	0	0	0	0	0	0	0
Steve Tandy	16	11	1	4	5	1	0	0	0	0	0
Stefan Terblanche	14	13	1	4	20	4	0	0	0	0	0
Jonathan Thomas	19	14	1	4	5	1	0	0	0	0	1
Dave Tiueti	11	8	1	2	10	2	0	0	0	0	0
Chris Wells	1	0	0	1	0	0	0	0	0	0	0
Rhodri Wells	1	1	0	0	0	0	0	0	0	0	0
Andy Williams	5	3	0	2	0	0	0	0	0	0	0
Barry Williams	25	19	1	5	5	1	0	0	0	0	0
Shane Williams	21	16	0	5	30	6	0	0	0	0	0

2005–06 Seasons Results & Player Stats

Date	Team 1			Team 2	Venue	
26/08/05	Ospreys	10	18	London Wasps	Liberty Stadium	
04/09/05	Ospreys	22	20	Leinster	Liberty Stadium	Tries: Andrew Bishop (2), Barry Williams; Cons: Matt Jones (2); Pens: Matt Jones
10/09/05	Munster	37	10	Ospreys	Musgrave Park	Tries: Barry Williams; Cons: Shaun Connor; Pens: Matt Jones
13/09/05	Ospreys	15	9	Newport Gwent Dragons	Liberty Stadium	Tries: Aled Brew, Penalty Try; Cons: Matt Jones; Pens: Matt Jones
18/09/05	Border Reivers	16	6	Ospreys	Netherdale Stadium	Pens: Shaun Connor (2)
25/09/05	Edinburgh Rugby	24	18	Ospreys	Murrayfield	Tries: Matt Jones, Stefan Terblanche; Cons: Matt Jones; Pens: Matt Jones (2)
01/10/05	Gloucester Rugby	23	7	Ospreys	Kingsholm	Tries: Steve Tandy, Cons: Matt Jones
09/10/05	Ospreys	20	27	Bath Rugby	Liberty Stadium	Tries: Matt Jones, Penalty Try; Cons: Matt Jones (2); Pens: Matt Jones, Shaun Connor
14/10/05	Ospreys	18	17	Connacht	Liberty Stadium	Pens: Shaun Connor (5), Matt Jones
23/10/05	Ospreys	13	8	Stade Français Paris	Liberty Stadium	Tries: Sonny Parker; Cons: Shaun Connor; Pens: Matt Jones, Shaun Connor
30/10/05	ASM Clermont Auvergne	34	14	Ospreys	Stade Marcel Michelin	Tries: Shane Williams; Pens: Shaun Connor (2); DG: Shaun Connor
04/11/05	Ulster	12	20	Ospreys	Ravenhill	Tries: Jason Spice; Pens: Shaun Connor (4); DG: Shaun Connor
04/12/05	Bristol Rugby	28	43	Ospreys	Memorial Ground	Tries: Adrian Cashmore (2), Damian Karauna, James Bater, Steve Tandy; Cons: Shaun Connor (2), Matt Jones; Pens: Shaun Connor (4)
11/12/05	Leicester Tigers	30	12	Ospreys	Welford Road	Tries: Adrian Cashmore, Sonny Parker; Cons: Shaun Connor
18/12/05	Ospreys	15	17	Leicester Tigers	Liberty Stadium	Tries: Barry Williams, Shaun Connor; Cons: Shaun Connor; Pens: Shaun Connor
22/12/05	Ospreys	9	28	Cardiff Blues	Liberty Stadium	Pens: Shaun Connor (2), Adrian Cashmore
01/01/06	Newport Gwent Dragons	24	14	Ospreys	Rodney Parade	Tries: Shaun Connor; Pens: Adrian Cashmore (3)
14/01/06	Ospreys	26	12	ASM Clermont Auvergne	Liberty Stadium	Tries: Richard Mustoe, Stefan Terblanche; Cons: Adrian Cashmore (2); Pens: Adrian Cashmore (4)
20/01/06	Stade Français Paris	43	10	Ospreys	Stade Jean Bouin	Tries: Matt Jones; Cons: Matt Jones; Pens: Shaun Connor
27/01/06	Glasgow Warriors	8	22	Ospreys	Old Anniesland	Tries: Adrian Cashmore; Cons: Adrian Cashmore; Pens: Shaun Connor (3), Adrian Cashmore; DG: Shaun Connor
17/02/06	Ospreys	22	18	Border Reivers	Liberty Stadium	Tries: Andrew Bishop; Cons: Gavin Henson; Pens: Gavin Henson (4); DG: Shaun Connor
03/03/06	Cardiff Blues	40	14	Ospreys	Cardiff Arms Park	Tries: James Bater; Pens: Gavin Henson; DG: Shaun Connor (2)
26/03/06	Ospreys	24	17	Edinburgh Rugby	Liberty Stadium	Tries: Huw Bennett, Shaun Connor; Cons: Gavin Henson; Pens: Gavin Henson (4)
31/03/06	Scarlets	30	17	Ospreys	Stradey Park	Tries: Stefan Terblanche; Pens: Gavin Henson (4)
08/04/06	Ospreys	16	13	Glasgow Warriors	Liberty Stadium	Tries: Richard Mustoe, Steve Tandy; Pens: Gavin Henson, Shaun Connor
18/04/06	Ospreys	25	13	Scarlets	Liberty Stadium	Tries: Penalty Try; Cons: Gavin Henson; Pens: Gavin Henson (5); DG: Gavin Henson
29/04/06	Leinster	38	21	Ospreys	Lansdowne Road	Tries: Gavin Henson, Jonny Vaughton; Cons: Gavin Henson; Pens: Gavin Henson (3)
05/05/06	Ospreys	27	10	Munster	Liberty Stadium	Tries: Shane Williams (2), Jason Spice; Cons: Gavin Henson (3); Pens: Gavin Henson (2)
12/05/06	Connacht	16	44	Ospreys	The Sportsground	Tries: Jonny Vaughton (3), Huw Bennett, Lee Beach, Shaun Connor, Sonny Parker; Cons: James Hook (2), Gavin Henson; Pen: Gavin Henson
26/05/06	Ospreys	17	19	Ulster	Liberty Stadium	Tries: Jason Spice, Jonny Vaughton; Cons: Gavin Henson (2); Pens: Gavin Henson

Player	P	W	D	L	Pts	Try	Con	Pen	DG	YC	RC
Lyndon Bateman	23	11	0	12	0	0	0	0	0	1	0
James Bater	19	9	0	10	10	2	0	0	0	1	0
Lee Beach	16	8	0	8	5	1	0	0	0	0	0
Huw Bennett	23	13	0	10	10	2	0	0	0	0	0
Andrew Bishop	23	11	0	12	15	3	0	0	0	0	0
Dai Bishop	1	0	0	1	0	0	0	0	0	0	0
Aled Brew	5	3	0	2	5	1	0	0	0	0	0
Adrian Cashmore	11	6	0	5	53	4	3	9	0	0	0
Brent Cockbain	8	3	0	5	0	0	0	0	0	0	0
Shaun Connor	25	12	0	13	131	4	6	27	6	1	0
Leigh Davies	14	7	0	7	0	0	0	0	0	0	0
Des Dillon	7	3	0	4	0	0	0	0	0	0	0
Ian Evans	20	9	0	11	0	0	0	0	0	0	0
Cai Griffiths	8	5	0	3	0	0	0	0	0	3	0
Gavin Henson	13	6	0	7	106	1	10	26	1	0	0
Richard Hibbard	11	5	0	6	0	0	0	0	0	1	0
James Hook	1	1	0	0	4	0	2	0	0	0	0
Paul James	15	8	0	7	0	0	0	0	0	0	0
Adam Jones	22	9	0	13	0	0	0	0	0	0	0
Alun Wyn Jones	15	10	0	5	0	0	0	0	0	2	0
Duncan Jones	23	10	0	13	0	0	0	0	0	2	0
Matt Jones	22	9	0	13	57	3	9	8	0	0	0
Ryan Jones	1	0	0	1	0	0	0	0	0	0	0
Damian Karauna	10	6	0	4	5	1	0	0	0	0	0
Andy Lloyd	10	7	0	3	0	0	0	0	0	0	0
Andrew Millward	18	8	0	10	0	0	0	0	0	0	0
Craig Mitchell	2	1	0	1	0	0	0	0	0	0	0
Richard Mustoe	26	12	0	14	10	2	0	0	0	1	0
Andrew Newman	21	7	0	14	0	0	0	0	0	1	0
Sonny Parker	25	11	0	14	15	3	0	0	0	0	0
Richie Pugh	15	6	0	9	0	0	0	0	0	1	0
Richie Rees	4	2	0	2	0	0	0	0	0	0	0
Martin Roberts	11	5	0	6	0	0	0	0	0	0	0
Jason Spice	27	13	0	14	15	3	0	0	0	0	0
Steve Tandy	17	10	0	7	20	4	0	0	0	0	0
Stefan Terblanche	25	12	0	13	10	2	0	0	0	0	0
Jonathan Thomas	18	9	0	9	0	0	0	0	0	3	0
Jonny Vaughton	8	2	0	6	25	5	0	0	0	0	0
Rhodri Wells	3	1	0	2	0	0	0	0	0	0	0
Barry Williams	18	7	0	11	15	3	0	0	0	0	0
Shane Williams	13	6	0	7	15	3	0	0	0	0	0

2006—07 Seasons Results & Player Stats

Date	Team 1			Team 2	Venue	
25/08/06	Ospreys	24	14	Harlequins	Liberty Stadium	
02/09/06	Ospreys	17	11	Edinburgh Rugby	Liberty Stadium	Tries: Lee Byrne; Pens: James Hook (4)
08/09/06	Connacht	15	10	Ospreys	The Sportsground	Tries: Justin Marshall; Cons: James Hook; Pens: James Hook
13/09/06	Ospreys	18	16	Cardiff Blues	Liberty Stadium	Tries: Richie Pugh, Ryan Jones, Shane Williams; Pens; Gavin Henson
15/09/06	Ospreys	30	13	Border Reivers	Liberty Stadium	Tries: Alun Wyn Jones, Stefan Terblanche, Tal Selley; Cons: James Hook (3); Pens: James Hook (2); DG: Shaun Connor
22/09/06	Ulster	43	7	Ospreys	Ravenhill	Tries: Lee Byrne; Cons James Hook
29/09/06	Ospreys	49	19	Gloucester Rugby	Liberty Stadium	Tries: Sonny Parker (2), Barry Williams, Gavin Henson, Justin Marshall, Shane Williams; Cons: Gavin Henson (5); Pens: Gavin Henson (3)
07/10/06	Bath Rugby	24	31	Ospreys	Recreation Ground	Tries: James Hook, Jonny Vaughton, Stefan Terblanche; Cons: Shaun Connor (2); Pens: Shaun Connor; DG: James Hook, Shaun Connor, Stefan Terblanche
13/10/06	Ospreys	26	9	Glasgow Warriors	Liberty Stadium	Tries: Nikki Walker, Shane Williams, Sonny Parker, Steve Tandy; Cons: Gavin Henson (3)
20/10/06	Ospreys	17	16	Sale Sharks	Liberty Stadium	Tries: Shane Williams (2); Cons: James Hook, Shaun Connor; Pens: Shaun Connor
28/10/06	Stade Français Paris	27	14	Ospreys	Stade Jean Bouin	Tries: Lee Byrne, Sonny Parker; Cons: Gavin Henson, James Hook
01/11/06	Ospreys	24	16	Australia	Liberty Stadium	Tries: Barry Williams, Richard Mustoe; Cons: Shaun Connor; Pens: Shaun Connor (3); DG: Shaun Connor
25/11/06	Munster	25	20	Ospreys	Thomond Park	Tries: Jonny Vaughton, Shaun Connor; Cons Shaun Connor (2); Pens: Shaun Connor (2)
02/12/06	Ospreys	34	3	Bristol Rugby	Liberty Stadium	Tries: Barry Williams, Huw Bennett, James Hook, Justin Marshall, Nikki Walker; Cons: James Hook (3); Pens: James Hook
09/12/06	Rugby Calvisano	27	50	Ospreys	Centro Sportivo San Michele	Tries: Justin Marshall (2), Shane Williams (2), Huw Bennett, James Hook, Lee Byrne, Sonny Parker; Cons: James Hook (5)
15/12/06	Ospreys	26	9	Rugby Calvisano	Liberty Stadium	Tries: Adam Jones, Andy Lloyd, Lee Byrne, Ryan Jones; Cons: James Hook (3)
23/12/06	Cardiff Blues	30	24	Ospreys	Cardiff Arms Park	Tries: Filo Tiatia, Ian Evans; Cons: Gavin Henson; Pens: Gavin Henson (4)
26/12/06	Ospreys	50	24	Scarlets	Liberty Stadium	Tries: Andy Lloyd, Lee Byrne, Lyndon Bateman, Nikki Walker, Ryan Jones; Cons: James Hook (4), Shaun Connor; Pens: James Hook (5)
31/12/06	Ospreys	12	6	Newport Gwent Dragons	Liberty Stadium	Pens: James Hook (3), Gavin Henson
06/01/07	Leinster	45	22	Ospreys	Donnybrook	Tries: Brent Cockbain, Richie Pugh, Stefan Terblanche; Cons: Shaun Connor (2); Pens: Shaun Connor
14/01/07	Ospreys	22	22	Stade Français Paris	Liberty Stadium	Tries: Nikki Walker; Cons: James Hook; Pens: James Hook (5)
20/01/07	Sale Sharks	7	18	Ospreys	Edgeley Park	Tries: Stefan Terblanche, Steve Tandy; Cons: James Hook; Pens: Gavin Henson, James Hook
27/01/07	Ospreys	29	22	Ulster	Liberty Stadium	Tries: Nikki Walker (2); Cons: Shaun Connor (2); Pens: Shaun Connor (3); DG: Shaun Connor (2)
17/02/07	Ospreys	31	10	Connacht	Liberty Stadium	Tries: Lee Byrne, Paul James, Penalty Try; Cons: Lee Byrne (2); Pens: Lee Byrne (2), Shaun Connor; DG: Shane Williams
02/03/07	Edinburgh Rugby	12	30	Ospreys	Murrayfield	Tries: Huw Bennett, Jonny Vaughton, Justin Marshall, Stefan Terblanche, Steve Tandy; Cons: Jason Spice; Pens: Stefan Terblanche
24/03/07	Ospreys	27	10	Cardiff Blues	Millennium Stadium	Tries: Lee Byrne, Sonny Parker; Cons: James Hook; Pens: James Hook (4); DG: James Hook
07/04/07	Ospreys	20	12	Munster	Liberty Stadium	Tries: James Hook, Justin Marshall; Cons: James Hook (2); Pens: James Hook (2)
15/04/07	Leicester Tigers	41	35	Ospreys	Twickenham	Tries: Shane Williams (2), Lee Byrne, Nikki Walker; Cons: James Hook (3); Pens: James Hook (3)
24/04/07	Scarlets	6	19	Ospreys	Stradey Park	Tries: James Hook; Cons: James Hook; Pens: James Hook (3); DG: James Hook
27/04/07	Ospreys	19	17	Leinster	Liberty Stadium	Tries: Justin Marshall; Cons: Shaun Connor; Pens: James Hook (3), Shaun Connor
04/05/07	Glasgow Warriors	29	26	Ospreys	Hughenden	Tries: Shane Williams (2), Lee Byrne; Cons: James Hook; Pens: James Hook (2), Shaun Connor
08/05/07	Newport Gwent Dragons	13	27	Ospreys	Rodney Parade	Tries: Shane Williams (2), Andy Lloyd, Filo Tiatia; Cons: James Hook (2); Pens: Shaun Connor
12/05/07	Border Reivers	16	24	Ospreys	Netherdale Stadium	Tries: Sonny Parker (2), Filo Tiatia; Cons: James Hook (3); Pens: James Hook

Player	P	W	D	L	Pts	Try	Con	Pen	DG	YC	RC
Lyndon Bateman	12	10	0	2	5	1	0	0	0	0	0
Lee Beach	9	6	0	3	0	0	0	0	0	0	0
Huw Bennett	20	16	0	4	15	3	0	0	0	0	0
Andrew Bishop	28	20	1	7	0	0	0	0	0	0	0
Lee Byrne	24	16	1	7	60	10	2	2	0	0	0
Brent Cockbain	26	17	1	8	5	1	0	0	0	1	0
Shaun Connor	21	16	1	4	75	1	11	12	4	0	0
Ian Evans	10	7	0	3	5	1	0	0	0	1	0
Cai Griffiths	13	10	0	3	0	0	0	0	0	0	0
Gavin Henson	17	12	1	4	55	1	10	10	0	0	0
Richard Hibbard	9	7	0	2	0	0	0	0	0	0	0
James Hook	25	17	1	7	228	5	37	40	3	1	0
Paul James	25	17	1	7	5	1	0	0	0	0	0
Adam Jones	23	15	1	7	5	1	0	0	0	1	0
Alun Wyn Jones	25	18	1	6	5	1	0	0	0	1	0
Duncan Jones	22	16	1	5	0	0	0	0	0	0	0
Matt Jones	1	1	0	0	0	0	0	0	0	0	0
Ryan Jones	19	13	1	5	15	3	0	0	0	1	0
Ben Lewis	1	0	0	1	0	0	0	0	0	0	0
Andy Lloyd	18	13	1	4	15	3	0	0	0	2	0
Justin Marshall	26	18	1	7	40	8	0	0	0	2	0
Chris Martenko	2	1	0	1	0	0	0	0	0	0	0
Andrew Millward	11	9	0	2	0	0	0	0	0	0	0
Richard Mustoe	8	5	0	3	0	0	0	0	0	0	0
Sonny Parker	22	16	0	6	40	8	0	0	0	0	0
Mike Powell	14	9	1	4	0	0	0	0	0	2	0
Richie Pugh	17	10	0	7	10	2	0	0	0	0	0
Martin Roberts	6	5	0	1	0	0	0	0	0	0	0
Tal Selley	12	10	0	2	5	1	0	0	0	0	0
Ed Shervington	4	2	0	2	0	0	0	0	0	0	0
Tom Smith	2	2	0	0	0	0	0	0	0	0	0
Jason Spice	23	15	1	7	2	0	1	0	0	3	0
Jonathan Spratt	1	0	0	1	0	0	0	0	0	0	0
Steve Tandy	18	15	1	2	15	3	0	0	0	0	0
Stefan Terblanche	20	13	1	6	31	5	0	1	1	0	0
Jonathan Thomas	22	18	0	4	0	0	0	0	0	1	0
Filo Tiatia	20	13	1	6	15	3	0	0	0	2	0
Jonny Vaughton	12	9	0	3	15	3	0	0	0	0	0
Nikki Walker	28	19	1	8	35	7	0	0	0	0	0
Barry Williams	26	18	1	7	10	2	0	0	0	1	0
Shane Williams	21	16	1	4	68	13	0	0	1	0	0

2007—08 Seasons Results & Player Stats

Date	Team 1			Team 2	Venue	
18/08/07	Newbury	15	43	Ospreys	Monks Lane	
24/08/07	Ospreys	27	15	Bristol Rugby	Liberty Stadium	
31/08/07	Cardiff Blues	17	15	Ospreys	Cardiff Arms Park	Pens: Shaun Connor (5)
11/09/07	Ospreys	9	14	Scarlets	Liberty Stadium	Pens: Shaun Connor (3)
21/09/07	Ulster	17	16	Ospreys	Ravenhill	Tries: Andrew Bishop; Cons: Shaun Connor; Pens: Shaun Connor (3)
30/09/07	Ospreys	37	23	Glasgow Warriors	Liberty Stadium	Tries: Lee Byrne (2), Ben Lewis; Cons: Shaun Connor (2); Pens: Shaun Connor (4); DG: Shaun Connor (2)
05/10/07	Edinburgh Rugby	13	13	Ospreys	Murrayfield	Tries: Jonny Vaughton; Cons: Gareth Owen; Pens: Gareth Owen, Shaun Connor
14/10/07	Ospreys	16	3	Munster	Liberty Stadium	Tries: Lee Byrne, Shane Williams; Pens: Gareth Owen (2)
27/10/07	Worcester Warriors	16	47	Ospreys	Sixways Stadium	Tries: Lee Byrne (2), Shane Williams (2), Mike Phillips, Nikki Walker, Sonny Parker; Cons: James Hook (4), Shaun Connor (2)
04/11/07	Ospreys	51	16	London Irish	Liberty Stadium	Tries: Shane Williams (3), Alun Wyn Jones, Ben Lewis, Jonathan Thomas, Mike Phillips; Cons: James Hook (4), Shaun Connor; Pens: James Hook (2)
10/11/07	Ospreys	22	15	CS Bourgoin-Jallieu Rugby	Liberty Stadium	Tries: Gavin Henson; Cons: James Hook; Pens: James Hook (5)
16/11/07	Gloucester Rugby	26	18	Ospreys	Kingsholm	Tries: Sonny Parker (2); Cons: James Hook; Pens: James Hook (2)
23/11/07	Ospreys	19	26	Leinster	Liberty Stadium	Tries: Gareth Owen; Cons: Shaun Connor; Pens: Shaun Connor (3); DG: Shaun Connor
02/12/07	Harlequins	8	19	Ospreys	Twickenham Stoop	Tries: Gavin Henson; Cons: Gavin Henson; Pens: Gavin Henson (4)
07/12/07	Ospreys	48	17	Ulster	Liberty Stadium	Tries: Nikki Walker (2), Alun Wyn Jones, Filo Tiatia, Justin Marshall, Lee Byrne, Sonny Parker; Cons: James Hook (5); Pens: James Hook
14/12/07	Ulster	8	16	Ospreys	Ravenhill	Tries: Justin Marshall; Cons: James Hook; Pens: James Hook (3)
27/12/07	Scarlets	17	12	Ospreys	Stradey Park	Pens: James Hook (4)
31/12/07	Ospreys	22	3	Cardiff Blues	Liberty Stadium	Tries: Huw Bennett; Cons: James Hook; Pens: James Hook (5)
05/01/08	Leinster	26	15	Ospreys	Royal Dublin Society	Tries: Ben Lewis, Shaun Connor; Cons: Shaun Connor; Pens: Shaun Connor
12/01/08	Ospreys	32	15	Gloucester Rugby	Liberty Stadium	Tries: Richard Hibbard, Shane Williams; Cons: James Hook (2); Pens: James Hook (6)
20/01/08	CS Bourgoin-Jallieu Rugby	21	28	Ospreys	Stade Pierre Rajon	Tries: Jonathan Thomas, Lee Byrne, Shane Williams; Cons: James Hook (2); Pens: James Hook (3)
16/02/08	Ospreys	37	7	Connacht	Liberty Stadium	Tries: Gareth Owen, Marty Holah, Mike Phillips, Nikki Walker; Cons: Gareth Owen (2), Shaun Connor (2); Pens: Shaun Connor (3)
29/02/08	Glasgow Warriors	9	6	Ospreys	Firhill	Pens: Shaun Connor (2)
22/03/08	Saracens	3	30	Ospreys	Millennium Stadium	Tries: Shane Williams (2), Filo Tiatia, Gavin Henson; Cons: James Hook (2); Pens: James Hook (2)
28/03/08	Ospreys	32	7	Ulster	Liberty Stadium	Tries: Shane Williams (2), James Hook, Nikki Walker; Cons: James Hook (3); Pens: James Hook (2)
06/04/08	Saracens	19	10	Ospreys	Vicarage Road	Tries: Paul James; Cons: James Hook; Pens: James Hook
12/04/08	Leicester Tigers	6	23	Ospreys	Twickenham	Tries: Alun Wyn Jones, Andrew Bishop; Cons: James Hook (2); Pens: James Hook (3)
19/04/08	Munster	9	8	Ospreys	Musgrave Park	Tries: Sonny Parker; Pens: James Hook
25/04/08	Ospreys	16	3	Newport Gwent Dragons	Liberty Stadium	Tries: Aled Brew; Cons: James Hook; Pens: James Hook (2); DG: Justin Marshall
02/05/08	Ospreys	18	19	Edinburgh Rugby	Liberty Stadium	Pens: James Hook (6)
06/05/08	Newport Gwent Dragons	18	10	Ospreys	Rodney Parade	Tries: Shaun Connor; Cons: Shaun Connor; Pens: Shaun Connor
09/05/08	Connacht	24	20	Ospreys	The Sportsground	Tries: Kristian Phillips, Martin Roberts; Cons: Dan Biggar, Shaun Connor; Pens: Dan Biggar, Shaun Connor

Player	P	W	D	L	Pts	Try	Con	Pen	DG	YC	RC
Lyndon Bateman	13	5	1	7	0	0	0	0	0	0	0
Ashley Beck	2	0	0	2	0	0	0	0	0	0	0
Huw Bennett	20	14	1	5	5	1	0	0	0	0	0
Leigh Bevan	2	0	0	2	0	0	0	0	0	0	0
Ryan Bevington	1	0	0	1	0	0	0	0	0	0	0
Dan Biggar	2	1	0	1	5	0	1	1	0	0	0
Andrew Bishop	20	12	0	8	10	2	0	0	0	0	0
Aled Brew	15	4	1	10	5	1	0	0	0	0	0
Lee Byrne	22	14	0	8	35	7	0	0	0	3	0
Brent Cockbain	3	1	0	2	0	0	0	0	0	0	0
Mike Collins	2	0	0	2	0	0	0	0	0	0	0
Shaun Connor	21	9	1	11	124	2	12	27	3	0	0
Ian Evans	19	14	1	4	0	0	0	0	0	0	0
Ian Gough	18	12	1	5	0	0	0	0	0	0	0
Cai Griffiths	18	6	1	11	0	0	0	0	0	0	0
Gavin Henson	13	9	1	3	29	3	1	4	0	1	0
Richard Hibbard	26	13	1	12	5	1	0	0	0	0	0
Marty Holah	19	12	0	7	5	1	0	0	0	1	0
James Hook	18	13	0	5	209	1	30	48	0	0	0
Paul James	24	13	1	10	5	1	0	0	0	2	0
Adam Jones	17	13	0	4	0	0	0	0	0	0	0
Alun Wyn Jones	19	13	0	6	15	3	0	0	0	0	0
Duncan Jones	19	14	0	5	0	0	0	0	0	0	0
Ryan Jones	10	7	0	3	0	0	0	0	0	0	0
Ben Lewis	16	8	1	7	15	3	0	0	0	0	0
Andy Lloyd	9	2	0	7	0	0	0	0	0	0	0
Justin Marshall	23	14	0	9	13	2	0	0	1	0	0
Andrew Millward	11	3	1	7	0	0	0	0	0	1	0
Craig Mitchell	1	0	0	1	0	0	0	0	0	0	0
Gareth Owen	12	4	1	7	25	2	3	3	0	1	0
Sonny Parker	17	12	0	5	25	5	0	0	0	0	0
Kristian Phillips	2	0	0	2	5	1	0	0	0	0	0
Mike Phillips	16	12	1	3	15	3	0	0	0	2	0
Mike Powell	7	1	0	6	0	0	0	0	0	0	0
Richie Pugh	2	0	0	2	0	0	0	0	0	0	0
Martin Roberts	9	3	1	5	5	1	0	0	0	0	0
Ed Shervington	9	3	0	6	0	0	0	0	0	0	0
Tom Smith	12	3	1	8	0	0	0	0	0	0	0
Jonathan Spratt	9	3	0	6	0	0	0	0	0	1	0
Steve Tandy	7	2	1	4	0	0	0	0	0	0	0
Mark Taylor	17	8	1	8	0	0	0	0	0	0	0
Stefan Terblanche	5	1	1	3	0	0	0	0	0	0	0
Adrian Thomas	2	0	0	2	0	0	0	0	0	0	0
Jonathan Thomas	17	12	0	5	10	2	0	0	0	0	0
Filo Tiatia	27	15	1	11	10	2	0	0	0	2	0
Hale T-Pole	8	4	0	4	0	0	0	0	0	1	0
Jonny Vaughton	21	9	1	11	5	1	0	0	0	2	0
Nikki Walker	17	12	0	5	25	5	0	0	0	0	0
Rhys Webb	4	1	0	3	0	0	0	0	0	1	0
Rhodri Wells	2	1	0	1	0	0	0	0	0	0	0
Barry Williams	5	2	0	3	0	0	0	0	0	0	0
Shane Williams	16	14	0	2	60	12	0	0	0	0	0

2008—09 Seasons Results & Player Stats

Date	Team 1			Team 2	Venue	
23/08/08	Ospreys	17	30	Leicester Tigers	Liberty Stadium	
30/08/08	Ospreys Select XV	0	66	Ospreys	The Old Parish Ground	
05/09/08	Connacht	3	16	Ospreys	The Sportsground	Tries: Nikki Walker; Cons: James Hook; Pens: James Hook (3)
09/09/08	Ospreys	32	10	Cardiff Blues	Liberty Stadium	Tries: James Hook (2), Shane Williams, Tommy Bowe; Cons: James Hook (3); Pens: James Hook (2)
12/09/08	Glasgow Warriors	18	21	Ospreys	Firhill	Tries: Alun Wyn Jones, Kristian Phillips, Cons: James Hook; Pens: Dan Biggar (2); DG: Dan Biggar
19/09/08	Leinster	19	13	Ospreys	Royal Dublin Society	Tries: Nikki Walker; Cons: James Hook; Pens: James Hook; DG: James Hook
27/09/08	Ospreys	43	0	Ulster	Liberty Stadium	Tries: James Hook, Lee Byrne, Rhodri Wells, Ryan Jones, Shane Williams, Tommy Bowe; Cons: James Hook (5); Pens: James Hook
05/10/08	Ospreys	24	23	Harlequins	Liberty Stadium	Tries: Shane Williams, Tommy Bowe; Cons: James Hook; Pens: James Hook (4)
12/10/08	Leicester Tigers	12	6	Ospreys	Welford Road	Pens: James Hook; DG: Shane Williams
18/10/08	Ospreys	15	9	USA Perpignan	Liberty Stadium	Pens: Dan Biggar (5)
26/10/08	Ospreys	37	22	Worcester Warriors	Liberty Stadium	Tries: Gavin Henson, Nikki Walker, Shane Williams, Tommy Bowe; Cons: James Hook; Pens: James Hook (5)
02/11/08	London Irish	23	19	Ospreys	Madejski Stadium	Tries: Nikki Walker; Cons: James Hook; Pens: James Hook (4)
28/11/08	Edinburgh Rugby	32	16	Ospreys	Murrayfield	Tries: Nikki Walker; Cons: Matthew Jarvis; Pens: Matthew Jarvis (3)
06/12/08	Ospreys	68	8	Benetton Rugby Treviso	Liberty Stadium	Tries: Tommy Bowe (4), Nikki Walker (2), Ed Shervington, Jonathan Thomas, Lee Byrne, Shane Williams; Cons: James Hook (9)
13/12/08	Benetton Rugby Treviso	16	36	Ospreys	Stadio Comunale di Monigo	Tries: Sonny Parker (2), Alun Wyn Jones, Filo Tiatia, Jonathan Thomas; Cons: James Hook (3), Dan Biggar; Pens: James Hook
19/12/08	Newport Gwent Dragons	30	24	Ospreys	Rodney Parade	Tries: Gavin Henson (2); Cons: Dan Biggar; Pens: Dan Biggar (4)
27/12/08	Ospreys	20	6	Scarlets	Liberty Stadium	Tries: Mike Phillips, Ryan Jones; Cons: James Hook (2); Pens: James Hook (2)
31/12/08	Cardiff Blues	12	16	Ospreys	Cardiff Arms Park	Tries: Filo Tiatia, Lee Byrne; Pens: Dan Biggar, James Hook
09/01/09	Ospreys	21	25	Munster	Liberty Stadium	Pens: James Hook (7)
17/01/09	USA Perpignan	17	15	Ospreys	Stade Aimé Giral	Tries: Jonny Vaughton, Shane Williams; Cons: James Hook; Pens: James Hook
24/01/09	Ospreys	15	9	Leicester Tigers	Liberty Stadium	Pens: James Hook (5)
22/02/09	Ospreys	22	10	Connacht	Liberty Stadium	Tries: Jonathan Spratt, Jonny Vaughton, Steve Tandy; Cons: Dan Biggar (2); Pens: Dan Biggar
06/03/09	Ospreys	8	13	Leinster	Liberty Stadium	Tries: Sonny Parker; DG: Dan Biggar
28/03/09	Gloucester Rugby	17	0	Ospreys	Ricoh Arena	
03/04/09	Ulster	13	16	Ospreys	Ravenhill	Tries: Filo Tiatia; Cons: James Hook; Pens: James Hook (3)
12/04/09	Munster	43	9	Ospreys	Thomond Park	Pens: James Hook (3)
18/04/09	Scarlets	19	28	Ospreys	Parc y Scarlets	Tries: Lee Byrne, Ryan Jones, Shane Williams; Cons: James Hook (2): Pens: Dan Biggar (2), James Hook
25/04/09	Ospreys	30	32	Edinburgh Rugby	Liberty Stadium	Tries: Huw Bennett, Lee Byrne, Shane Williams, Tommy Bowe; Cons: Dan Biggar (2); Pens: Dan Biggar (2)
30/04/09	Ospreys	27	18	Newport Gwent Dragons	Liberty Stadium	Tries: James Hook, Shane Williams; Cons: James Hook; Pens: James Hook (3); DG: Dan Biggar, James Hook
10/05/09	Ospreys	34	23	Glasgow Warriors	Liberty Stadium	Tries: Filo Tiatia, Gareth Owen, Jamie Nutbrown; Cons: James Hook (2); Pens: James Hook (5)
15/05/09	Munster	36	10	Ospreys	Thomond Park	Tries: James Hook; Cons: James Hook; Pens: James Hook

Player	P	W	D	L	Pts	Try	Con	Pen	DG	YC	RC
Scott Baldwin	2	0	0	2	0	0	0	0	0	0	0
Lyndon Bateman	5	2	0	3	0	0	0	0	0	0	0
Ashley Beck	5	2	0	3	0	0	0	0	0	0	0
Huw Bennett	18	10	0	8	5	1	0	0	0	1	0
Ryan Bevington	2	1	0	1	0	0	0	0	0	0	0
Dan Biggar	20	11	0	9	72	0	6	17	3	0	0
Andrew Bishop	21	11	0	10	0	0	0	0	0	1	0
Dai Bishop	6	3	0	3	0	0	0	0	0	0	0
Tommy Bowe	22	13	0	9	45	9	0	0	0	0	0
Marc Breeze	1	0	0	1	0	0	0	0	0	0	0
Lee Byrne	17	12	0	5	25	5	0	0	0	2	0
David Evans	1	0	0	1	0	0	0	0	0	0	0
Ian Evans	6	4	0	2	0	0	0	0	0	0	0
Rhys Garfield	1	0	0	1	0	0	0	0	0	0	0
Ian Gough	22	13	0	9	0	0	0	0	0	0	0
Cai Griffiths	15	8	0	7	0	0	0	0	0	0	0
Gavin Henson	10	6	0	4	15	3	0	0	0	0	0
Richard Hibbard	20	13	0	7	0	0	0	0	0	0	0
Marty Holah	26	15	0	11	0	0	0	0	0	1	0
James Hook	24	15	0	9	265	5	36	54	2	0	0
Paul James	27	15	0	12	0	0	0	0	0	2	0
Matthew Jarvis	1	0	0	1	11	0	1	3	0	0	0
Adam Jones	20	12	0	8	0	0	0	0	0	0	0
Alun Wyn Jones	22	15	0	7	10	2	0	0	0	0	0
Duncan Jones	13	9	0	4	0	0	0	0	0	0	0
Ryan Jones	21	12	0	9	15	3	0	0	0	2	0
Richard Kelly	1	0	0	1	0	0	0	0	0	0	0
Tavis Knoyle	1	1	0	0	0	0	0	0	0	0	0
Filipo Levi	8	5	0	3	0	0	0	0	0	0	0
Andy Lloyd	10	5	0	5	0	0	0	0	0	0	0
Andrew Millward	1	1	0	0	0	0	0	0	0	0	0
Craig Mitchell	3	0	0	3	0	0	0	0	0	0	0
Jamie Nutbrown	14	9	0	5	5	1	0	0	0	1	0
Gareth Owen	9	7	0	2	5	1	0	0	0	0	0
Sonny Parker	18	11	0	7	15	3	0	0	0	0	0
Kristian Phillips	4	2	0	2	5	1	0	0	0	0	0
Mike Phillips	12	6	0	6	5	1	0	0	0	1	0
Ed Shervington	13	9	0	4	5	1	0	0	0	0	0
Tom Smith	21	13	0	8	0	0	0	0	0	1	0
Jonathan Spratt	8	4	0	4	5	1	0	0	0	0	0
Steve Tandy	15	9	0	6	5	1	0	0	0	1	0
Jonathan Thomas	12	7	0	5	10	2	0	0	0	0	0
Filo Tiatia	26	15	0	11	20	4	0	0	0	2	0
Jonny Vaughton	14	8	0	6	10	2	0	0	0	0	0
Nikki Walker	10	6	0	4	35	7	0	0	0	0	0
Rhys Webb	12	9	0	3	0	0	0	0	0	0	0
Rhodri Wells	11	5	0	6	5	1	0	0	0	0	0
Shane Williams	18	11	0	7	48	9	0	0	1	0	0

2009—10 Seasons Results & Player Stats

Date	Team 1			Team 2	Venue	
22/08/09	Ospreys	35	20	Leeds Carnegie	Liberty Stadium	
29/08/09	Gloucester Rugby	16	22	Ospreys	Kingsholm	
04/09/09	Connacht	12	19	Ospreys	The Sportsground	Tries: Jerry Collins; Cons: Dan Biggar; Pens: Dan Biggar (2), James Hook; DG: Dan Biggar
12/09/09	Ospreys	16	20	Ulster	Liberty Stadium	Tries: Duncan Jones, Nikki Walker; Pens: James Hook (2)
18/09/09	Ospreys	11	18	Leinster	Liberty Stadium	Tries: Jerry Collins; Pens: James Hook (2)
25/09/09	Glasgow Warriors	16	26	Ospreys	Firhill	Tries: Nikki Walker, Tommy Bowe; Cons: Dan Biggar (2); Pens: Dan Biggar (3); DG: Dan Biggar
04/10/09	Ospreys	31	10	Edinburgh Rugby	Liberty Stadium	Tries: Jonathan Thomas, Lee Byrne, Ryan Jones, Tommy Bowe; Cons: Dan Biggar (4); Pens: Dan Biggar
11/10/09	Leicester Tigers	32	32	Ospreys	Welford Road	Tries: Shane Williams, Tommy Bowe; Cons: Dan Biggar (2); Pens: Dan Biggar (5); DG: Dan Biggar
18/10/09	Ospreys	25	24	ASM Clermont Auvergne	Liberty Stadium	Tries: Barry Davies, Ryan Jones, Tommy Bowe; Cons: Dan Biggar (2); Pens: Dan Biggar; DG: James Hook
24/10/09	Cardiff Blues	20	12	Ospreys	Cardiff City Stadium	Tries: Jerry Collins, Tommy Bowe; Cons: Dan Biggar
30/10/09	Ospreys	9	9	Glasgow Warriors	Liberty Stadium	Pens: Gareth Owen (3)
05/11/09	Ospreys	17	19	Northampton Saints	Liberty Stadium	Tries: Jonathan Spratt, Richard Hibbard; Cons: Gareth Owen (2); Pens: Gareth Owen
14/11/09	Bath Rugby	21	11	Ospreys	Recreation Ground	Tries: Justin Tipuric; Pens: Barry Davies, Gareth Owen
05/12/09	Ospreys	19	14	Munster	Liberty Stadium	Tries: Tommy Bowe; Cons: Dan Biggar; Pens: Dan Biggar (3); DG: Dan Biggar
12/12/09	Rugby Viadana	7	62	Ospreys	Stadio Giglio	Tries: Richard Hibbard (2), Alun Wyn Jones, Gareth Owen, Jerry Collins, Nikki Walker, Ricky Januarie, Tommy Bowe; Cons: Dan Biggar (8); Pens: Dan Biggar (2)
19/12/09	Ospreys	45	19	Rugby Viadana	Liberty Stadium	Tries: Tommy Bowe (2), Filo Tiatia, Gareth Owen, Nikki Walker, Sonny Parker; Cons: Dan Biggar (6); Pens: Dan Biggar
26/12/09	Scarlets	14	21	Ospreys	Parc y Scarlets	Tries: Paul James (2); Cons: Dan Biggar; Pens: Dan Biggar (3)
01/01/10	Ospreys	26	0	Cardiff Blues	Liberty Stadium	Tries: Nikki Walker (2), Ryan Jones; Cons: Dan Biggar; Pens: Dan Biggar (2); DG: Dan Biggar
16/01/10	ASM Clermont Auvergne	27	7	Ospreys	Stade Marcel Michelin	Tries: Tommy Bowe; Cons: Dan Biggar
23/01/10	Ospreys	17	12	Leicester Tigers	Liberty Stadium	Tries: Tommy Bowe; Pens: Dan Biggar (3); DG: Dan Biggar
29/01/10	Newport Gwent Dragons	40	19	Ospreys	Rodney Parade	Tries: Gareth Owen, Tom Prydie, Penalty Try; Cons: Tom Prydie (2)
04/02/10	Ospreys	21	17	Leeds Carnegie	Liberty Stadium	Tries: Hanno Dirksen, Jamie Nutbrown, Steve Tandy; Cons: Tom Prydie (3)
21/02/10	Ospreys	19	17	Connacht	Liberty Stadium	Tries: Dan Biggar, Gareth Owen; Pens: Dan Biggar (3)
07/03/10	Edinburgh Rugby	33	17	Ospreys	Murrayfield	Tries: Jerry Collins, Nikki Walker, Sonny Parker; Cons: Dan Biggar
27/03/10	Newport Gwent Dragons	28	20	Ospreys	Rodney Parade	Tries: Andrew Bishop, James Hook; Cons: Dan Biggar, James Hook; Pens: Dan Biggar (2)
02/04/10	Ospreys	27	19	Scarlets	Liberty Stadium	Tries: Tommy Bowe (2); Cons: Dan Biggar; Pens: Dan Biggar (3); DG: Dan Biggar (2)
10/04/10	Biarritz Olympique PB	29	28	Ospreys	Estadio Anoeta	Tries: Lee Byrne, Nikki Walker, Ryan Jones; Cons: Dan Biggar (2); Pens: Dan Biggar (2); DG: Dan Biggar
13/04/10	Ulster	27	38	Ospreys	Ravenhill	Tries: James Hook (2), Shane Williams, Tommy Bowe; Cons: Dan Biggar (3); Pens: Dan Biggar (4)
16/04/10	Leinster	20	16	Ospreys	Royal Dublin Society	Tries: Dan Biggar; Cons: Dan Biggar; Pens: Dan Biggar (3)
24/04/10	Munster	11	15	Ospreys	Thomond Park	Pens: Dan Biggar (5)
07/05/10	Ospreys	42	10	Newport Gwent Dragons	Liberty Stadium	Tries: Dan Biggar, Nikki Walker, Ryan Bevington, Ryan Jones, Penalty Try; Cons: Dan Biggar (4); Pens: Dan Biggar (3)
14/05/10	Ospreys	20	5	Glasgow Warriors	Liberty Stadium	Tries: James Hook, Shane Williams; Cons: Dan Biggar (2); Pens: Dan Biggar (2)
29/05/10	Leinster	12	17	Ospreys	Royal Dublin Society	Tries: Lee Byrne, Tommy Bowe; Cons: Dan Biggar (2); Pens: Dan Biggar

Player	P	W	D	L	Pts	Try	Con	Pen	DG	YC	RC
Ashley Beck	6	2	0	4	0	0	0	0	0	0	0
Huw Bennett	21	15	1	5	0	0	0	0	0	0	0
Ryan Bevington	14	8	1	5	5	1	0	0	0	2	0
Dan Biggar	26	17	1	8	298	3	47	54	9	0	0
Andrew Bishop	26	14	2	10	5	1	0	0	0	0	0
Tommy Bowe	23	15	2	6	75	15	0	0	0	1	0
Marc Breeze	1	0	0	1	0	0	0	0	0	0	0
Lee Byrne	16	11	1	4	15	3	0	0	0	0	0
Jerry Collins	29	17	2	10	25	5	0	0	0	2	0
Barry Davies	7	2	1	4	8	1	0	1	0	0	0
Liam Davies	4	1	1	2	0	0	0	0	0	0	0
Ross Davies	2	0	0	2	0	0	0	0	0	0	0
Hanno Dirksen	2	1	0	1	5	1	0	0	0	0	0
Ian Evans	8	5	0	3	0	0	0	0	0	1	0
James Goode	2	0	0	2	0	0	0	0	0	0	0
Ian Gough	24	13	2	9	0	0	0	0	0	2	0
Cai Griffiths	17	9	2	6	0	0	0	0	0	0	0
Richard Hibbard	20	11	2	7	15	3	0	0	0	1	0
Marty Holah	24	16	1	7	0	0	0	0	0	0	0
James Hook	21	13	1	7	40	4	1	5	1	0	0
Paul James	23	15	1	7	10	2	0	0	0	0	0
Matthew Jarvis	2	0	0	2	0	0	0	0	0	0	0
Adam Jones	14	10	0	4	0	0	0	0	0	1	0
Alun Wyn Jones	20	14	1	5	5	1	0	0	0	1	0
Duncan Jones	8	5	0	3	5	1	0	0	0	1	0
Ryan Jones	21	14	1	6	25	5	0	0	0	0	0
Richard Kelly	2	1	0	1	0	0	0	0	0	0	0
James King	4	0	1	3	0	0	0	0	0	0	0
Ben Lewis	1	1	0	0	0	0	0	0	0	0	0
Andy Lloyd	5	4	0	1	0	0	0	0	0	1	0
Craig Mitchell	12	8	1	3	0	0	0	0	0	0	0
Jamie Nutbrown	15	9	0	6	0	0	0	0	0	0	0
Gareth Owen	18	11	1	6	39	4	2	5	0	0	0
Sonny Parker	23	12	2	9	10	2	0	0	0	1	0
Kristian Phillips	2	0	0	2	0	0	0	0	0	0	0
Mike Phillips	18	11	1	6	0	0	0	0	0	1	0
Tom Prydie	1	1	0	0	0	0	0	0	0	0	0
Ed Shervington	12	6	0	6	0	0	0	0	0	1	0
Tom Smith	13	6	1	6	0	0	0	0	0	0	0
Jonathan Spratt	5	3	0	2	5	1	0	0	0	0	0
Steve Tandy	8	2	1	5	5	1	0	0	0	0	0
Jonathan Thomas	21	14	1	6	5	1	0	0	0	0	0
Nicky Thomas	3	0	1	2	0	0	0	0	0	0	0
Filo Tiatia	25	15	2	8	5	1	0	0	0	0	0
Justin Tipuric	2	0	0	2	5	1	0	0	0	0	0
Jonny Vaughton	7	3	0	4	0	0	0	0	0	0	0
Nikki Walker	26	16	2	8	45	9	0	0	0	0	0
Rhys Webb	3	1	0	2	0	0	0	0	0	0	0
Rhodri Wells	2	0	1	1	0	0	0	0	0	0	0
Shane Williams	16	10	1	5	15	3	0	0	0	0	0

2010—11 Seasons Results & Player Stats

Date	Team 1			Team 2	Venue	
10/08/10	Ospreys Select XV	22	58	Ospreys	Talbot Athletic Ground	
14/08/10	Leeds Carnegie	28	31	Ospreys	Headingley Carnegie	
21/08/10	Ospreys	14	24	Gloucester Rugby	Liberty Stadium	
03/09/10	Ulster	27	26	Ospreys	Ravenhill	Tries: Dan Biggar, Richard Fussell; Cons: Dan Biggar (2); Pens: Dan Biggar (4)
10/09/10	Ospreys	32	16	Benetton Rugby Treviso	Liberty Stadium	Tries: Andrew Bishop, Jonathan Thomas, Lee Byrne, Nikki Walker, Shane Williams; Cons: Dan Biggar (2); Pens: Dan Biggar
18/09/10	Munster	22	10	Ospreys	Thomond Park	Tries: Richard Fussell, Tommy Bowe
25/09/10	Ospreys	38	6	Aironi Rugby	Liberty Stadium	Tries: Lee Byrne, Richard Fussell, Tommy Bowe, Penalty Try; Cons: Dan Biggar (4), Gareth Owen; Pens: Dan Biggar
02/10/10	Scarlets	18	21	Ospreys	Parc y Scarlets	Tries: Alun Wyn Jones, Richard Fussell; Cons: Dan Biggar; Pens: Dan Biggar (2); DG: Dan Biggar
09/10/10	RC Toulonnais	19	14	Ospreys	Stade Félix Mayol	Tries: Shane Williams; Pens: Dan Biggar (3)
15/10/10	Ospreys	27	16	London Irish	Liberty Stadium	Tries: Shane Williams, Tommy Bowe; Cons: James Hook; Pens: Dan Biggar (4), James Hook
24/10/10	Glasgow Warriors	31	23	Ospreys	Firhill	Tries: Nikki Walker (3); Cons: Dan Biggar; Pens: Dan Biggar (2)
30/10/10	Ospreys	16	21	Newport Gwent Dragons	Liberty Stadium	Tries: Gareth Owen; Cons: Dai Flanagan; Pens: Dai Flanagan (2), Gareth Owen
06/11/10	Newcastle Falcons	18	17	Ospreys	Kingston Park	Tries: Gareth Owen; Pens: Matthew Morgan (4)
12/11/10	Ospreys	46	13	Leicester Tigers	Riverside Hardware Brewery Field	Tries: Kristian Phillips (2), Ashley Beck, Matthew Morgan, Rhys Webb, Richard Fussell, Sonny Parker, Penalty Try; Cons: Gareth Owen, Matthew Morgan, Tom Prydie
19/11/10	Connacht	15	16	Ospreys	The Sportsground	Tries: Jamie Nutbrown; Cons: Matthew Jarvis; Pens: Matthew Morgan (2); DG: Matthew Morgan
28/11/10	Ospreys	19	15	Leinster	Liberty Stadium	Tries: Penalty Try; Cons: Dan Biggar; Pens: Dan Biggar (4)
04/12/10	Ospreys	33	16	Edinburgh Rugby	Liberty Stadium	Tries: Justin Tipuric, Richard Fussell; Cons: Dan Biggar; Pens: Dan Biggar (6); DG: Dan Biggar
12/12/10	Munster	22	16	Ospreys	Thomond Park	Tries: Tommy Bowe; Cons: Dan Biggar; Pens: Dan Biggar (3)
18/12/10	Ospreys	19	15	Munster	Liberty Stadium	Tries: Mike Phillips; Cons: Dan Biggar; Pens: Dan Biggar (4)
27/12/10	Ospreys	60	17	Scarlets	Liberty Stadium	Tries: Dan Biggar, James Hook, Jamie Nutbrown, Jonathan Thomas, Paul James, Richard Fussell, Tommy Bowe; Cons: Dan Biggar (3), James Hook (2); Pens: Dan Biggar (5)
31/12/10	Cardiff Blues	27	25	Ospreys	Cardiff City Stadium	Tries: Andrew Bishop, Paul James, Tommy Bowe; Cons: James Hook (2); Pens: Dan Biggar, James Hook
07/01/11	Leinster	15	10	Ospreys	Royal Dublin Society	Tries: Justin Tipuric; Cons: Dan Biggar; Pens: Dan Biggar
16/01/11	London Irish	24	12	Ospreys	Madejski Stadium	Pens: Dan Biggar (3), James Hook
22/01/11	Ospreys	29	17	RC Toulonnais	Liberty Stadium	Tries: Alun Wyn Jones, Nikki Walker; Cons: James Hook (2); Pens: Dan Biggar (3), James Hook (2)
29/01/11	Cardiff Blues	7	29	Ospreys	Cardiff City Stadium	Tries: Hanno Dirksen, Morgan Allen, Penalty Try; Cons: Matthew Morgan; Pens: Matthew Morgan (4)
06/02/11	Ospreys	18	13	London Wasps	Riverside Hardware Brewery Field	Pens: Dai Flanagan (4), Dan Biggar; DG: Dan Biggar
13/02/11	Ospreys	23	22	Ulster	Liberty Stadium	Tries: Marty Holah; Pens: Dan Biggar (6)
19/02/11	Benetton Rugby Treviso	18	34	Ospreys	Stadio Comunale di Monigo	Tries: Nikki Walker (3), Ashley Beck, Ian Gough; Cons: Dan Biggar (3); Pens: Dan Biggar
27/02/11	Ospreys	33	18	Connacht	Liberty Stadium	Tries: Mefin Davies, Richard Fussell, Sonny Parker, Tom Prydie; Cons: Dan Biggar (2); Pens: Dan Biggar (2); DG: Dan Biggar
05/03/11	Ospreys	37	6	Glasgow Warriors	Liberty Stadium	Tries: Ashley Beck, Dan Biggar, Jerry Collins, Tom Smith, Penalty Try; Cons: Dan Biggar (3); Pens: Dan Biggar; DG: Dan Biggar
26/03/11	Edinburgh Rugby	23	16	Ospreys	Murrayfield	Tries: Dan Biggar; Cons: Dan Biggar; Pens: Dan Biggar (3)
02/04/11	Ospreys	21	21	Cardiff Blues	Liberty Stadium	Pens: Dan Biggar (5); DG: Dan Biggar
15/04/11	Newport Gwent Dragons	32	28	Ospreys	Rodney Parade	Tries: Nikki Walker, Ryan Jones, Tommy Bowe; Cons: James Hook (2); Pens: Dan Biggar (2), James Hook
23/04/11	Ospreys	20	22	Munster	Liberty Stadium	Tries: Alun Wyn Jones, Penalty Try; Cons: Dan Biggar (2); Pens: Dan Biggar, James Hook
06/05/11	Aironi Rugby	10	12	Ospreys	Stadio Luigi Zaffanella	Pens: Dan Biggar (3), James Hook
14/05/11	Munster	18	11	Ospreys	Thomond Park	Tries: Richard Fussell; Pens: Dan Biggar (2)

Player	P	W	D	L	Pts	Try	Con	Pen	DG	YC	RC
Morgan Allen	1	1	0	0	5	1	0	0	0	0	0
Scott Baldwin	1	0	0	1	0	0	0	0	0	0	0
Ashley Beck	15	10	0	5	15	3	0	0	0	0	0
Huw Bennett	23	13	1	9	0	0	0	0	0	0	0
Ryan Bevington	20	10	1	9	0	0	0	0	0	0	0
Dan Biggar	28	15	1	12	318	4	29	74	6	0	0
Andrew Bishop	18	9	0	9	10	2	0	0	0	0	0
Tommy Bowe	19	8	1	10	35	7	0	0	0	0	0
Lee Byrne	13	5	1	7	10	2	0	0	0	0	0
Jerry Collins	27	14	1	12	5	1	0	0	0	4	0
Craig Cross	4	4	0	0	0	0	0	0	0	0	0
Barry Davies	12	6	0	6	0	0	0	0	0	0	0
Mefin Davies	14	7	0	7	5	1	0	0	0	0	0
Hanno Dirksen	5	5	0	0	5	1	0	0	0	0	0
Ian Evans	20	11	1	8	0	0	0	0	0	2	0
Dai Flanagan	5	4	0	1	20	0	1	6	0	0	0
Richard Fussell	29	15	1	13	45	9	0	0	0	0	0
James Goode	8	5	0	3	0	0	0	0	0	0	0
Ian Gough	27	15	1	11	5	1	0	0	0	1	0
Cai Griffiths	18	11	0	7	0	0	0	0	0	1	0
Richard Hibbard	22	11	1	10	0	0	0	0	0	1	0
Marty Holah	24	13	0	11	5	1	0	0	0	1	0
James Hook	17	7	1	9	50	1	9	8	1	0	0
Tom Isaacs	12	7	0	5	0	0	0	0	0	0	0
Paul James	19	8	1	10	10	2	0	0	0	2	0
Matthew Jarvis	2	1	0	1	2	0	1	0	0	0	0
Ben John	1	0	0	1	0	0	0	0	0	0	0
Adam Jones	19	8	1	10	0	0	0	0	0	0	0
Alun Wyn Jones	18	8	1	9	15	3	0	0	0	0	0
Duncan Jones	23	14	0	9	0	0	0	0	0	1	0
Ryan Jones	19	8	1	10	5	1	0	0	0	2	0
Richard Kelly	1	1	0	0	0	0	0	0	0	0	0
James King	9	8	0	1	0	0	0	0	0	0	0
Ben Lewis	4	2	0	2	0	0	0	0	0	0	0
Andy Lloyd	4	2	0	2	0	0	0	0	0	0	0
Matthew Morgan	5	4	0	1	42	1	2	10	1	0	0
Craig Mitchell	15	8	0	7	0	0	0	0	0	0	0
Conor McInerney	4	2	0	2	0	0	0	0	0	0	0
Jamie Nutbrown	19	12	0	7	10	2	0	0	0	0	0
Gareth Owen	11	7	0	4	17	2	2	1	0	0	0
Sonny Parker	21	10	1	10	10	2	0	0	0	0	0
Kristian Phillips	5	4	0	1	10	2	0	0	0	0	0
Mike Phillips	14	7	1	6	5	1	0	0	0	0	0
Tom Prydie	7	6	0	1	7	1	1	0	0	0	0
Joe Rees	2	2	0	0	0	0	0	0	0	0	0
Tom Smith	14	8	0	6	5	1	0	0	0	0	0
Will Taylor	1	1	0	0	0	0	0	0	0	0	0
Jonathan Thomas	19	10	0	9	10	2	0	0	0	0	0
Justin Tipuric	27	16	1	10	10	2	0	0	0	0	0
Eli Walker	1	1	0	0	0	0	0	0	0	0	0
Nikki Walker	21	8	1	12	45	9	0	0	0	1	0
Rhys Webb	21	12	1	8	5	1	0	0	0	0	0
Shane Williams	8	5	0	3	15	3	0	0	0	0	0

2011—12 Seasons Results & Player Stats

Date	Team 1			Team 2	Venue	
12/08/11	Lyon Olympique Universitaire	38	10	Ospreys	Stade Marius Berthe	
21/08/11	Ospreys	46	19	Russia	Liberty Stadium	
02/09/11	Ospreys	27	3	Leinster	Liberty Stadium	Tries: Hanno Dirksen, Justin Tipuric, Rhys Webb; Cons: Dan Biggar (3); Pens: Dan Biggar; DG: Dan Biggar
10/09/11	Ospreys	26	19	Edinburgh Rugby	Liberty Stadium	Tries: Justin Tipuric, Rhys Webb; Cons: Dan Biggar (2); Pens: Dan Biggar (4)
17/09/11	Benetton Rugby Treviso	27	32	Ospreys	Stadio Comunale di Monigo	Tries: Tom Isaacs, Tom Smith; Cons: Dan Biggar (2); Pens: Dan Biggar (4), Kristian Phillips; DG: Dan Biggar
25/09/11	Ospreys	32	14	Ulster	Liberty Stadium	Tries: Richard Fussell, Penalty Try; Cons: Dan Biggar, Matthew Morgan; Pens: Dan Biggar (6)
30/09/11	Ospreys	26	21	Connacht	Liberty Stadium	Tries: Barry Davies, Hanno Dirksen; Cons: Dan Biggar (2); Pens: Dan Biggar (4)
08/10/11	Munster	13	17	Ospreys	Thomond Park	Tries: Rhys Webb; Pens: Dan Biggar (4)
15/10/11	Exeter Chiefs	35	9	Ospreys	Sandy Park Stadium	Pens: Matthew Morgan (3)
22/10/11	Ospreys	22	32	Northampton Saints	Riverside Hardware Brewery Field	Tries: Sonny Parker; Cons: Matthew Morgan; Pens: Matthew Morgan (5)
28/10/11	Glasgow Warriors	28	17	Ospreys	Firhill	Tries: Matthew Morgan; Pens: Matthew Morgan (4)
05/11/11	Ospreys	9	9	Scarlets	Liberty Stadium	Pens: Dan Biggar (3)
12/11/11	Ospreys	28	21	Biarritz Olympique PB	Liberty Stadium	Tries: Tommy Bowe; Cons: Dan Biggar; Pens: Dan Biggar (7)
19/11/11	Benetton Rugby Treviso	26	26	Ospreys	Stadio Comunale di Monigo	Tries: Ryan Jones, Tommy Bowe; Cons: Dan Biggar (2); Pens: Dan Biggar (3), Matthew Morgan
26/11/11	Connacht	6	17	Ospreys	The Sportsground	Tries: Matthew Morgan, Sonny Parker; Cons: Matthew Morgan (2); Pens: Matthew Morgan
03/12/11	Ospreys	19	13	Munster	Liberty Stadium	Tries: Rhys Webb, Richard Fussell; Pens: Matthew Morgan (3)
10/12/11	Saracens	31	26	Ospreys	Wembley Stadium	Tries: Ashley Beck (2); Cons: Dan Biggar (2); Pens: Dan Biggar (4)
16/12/11	Ospreys	13	16	Saracens	Liberty Stadium	Tries: Ian Gough; Cons: Dan Biggar; Pens: Dan Biggar (2)
26/12/11	Scarlets	22	14	Ospreys	Parc y Scarlets	Tries: Barry Davies; Pens: Dan Biggar (3)
01/01/12	Ospreys	17	12	Cardiff Blues	Liberty Stadium	Tries: Tommy Bowe; Pens: Dan Biggar (2), Matthew Morgan (2)
06/01/12	Newport Gwent Dragons	21	20	Ospreys	Rodney Parade	Tries: Tommy Bowe; Pens: Matthew Morgan (4), Dan Biggar
13/01/12	Ospreys	44	17	Benetton Rugby Treviso	Liberty Stadium	Tries: Ashley Beck (2), Kahn Fotuali'I, Tommy Bowe, Penalty Try (2); Cons: Dan Biggar (3), Matthew Morgan; Pens: Dan Biggar (2)
22/01/12	Biarritz Olympique PB	36	5	Ospreys	Parc des Sports Aguiléra	Tries: Richard Hibbard
27/01/12	Ospreys	26	21	Newport Gwent Dragons	Riverside Hardware Brewery Field	Tries: Eli Walker, Hanno Dirksen, Ross Jones, Stefan Watermeyer; Cons: Matthew Morgan (3)
04/02/12	Worcester Warriors	24	14	Ospreys	Sixways Stadium	Tries: Hanno Dirksen, Matthew Morgan; Cons: Matthew Morgan (2)
10/02/12	Edinburgh Rugby	14	15	Ospreys	Murrayfield	Tries: Hanno Dirksen, Richard Hibbard; Cons: Dan Biggar; DG: Dan Biggar
17/02/12	Ospreys	23	7	Aironi Rugby	Liberty Stadium	Tries: Andrew Bishop, Penalty Try; Cons: Dan Biggar, Matthew Morgan; Pens: Dan Biggar (3)
24/02/12	Ulster	15	14	Ospreys	Ravenhill	Tries: Eli Walker, Joe Bearman; Cons: Dan Biggar (2)
02/03/12	Ospreys	20	26	Glasgow Warriors	Liberty Stadium	Tries: Hanno Dirksen, Kahn Fotuali'I; Cons: Dan Bigar (2); Pens: Dan Biggar (2)
23/03/12	Leinster	22	23	Ospreys	Royal Dublin Society	Tries: George Stowers, Richard Hibbard; Cons: Dan Biggar (2); Pens: Dan Biggar (3)
31/03/12	Ospreys	41	10	Benetton Rugby Treviso	Liberty Stadium	Tries: Ashley Beck (2), Joe Bearman, Paul James, Tom Isaacs; Cons: Dan Biggar (5); Pens: Dan Biggar (2)
14/04/12	Cardiff Blues	12	33	Ospreys	Cardiff City Stadium	Tries: Adam Jones, Alun Wyn Jones, Tom Smith; Cons: Dan Biggar (3); Pens: Dan Biggar (4)
20/04/12	Ospreys	31	12	Newport Gwent Dragons	Liberty Stadium	Tries: Ryan Jones, Shane Williams, Penalty Try (2); Cons: Dan Biggar (3), Shane Williams; Pens: Dan Biggar
05/05/12	Aironi Rugby	11	18	Ospreys	Stadio Luigi Zaffanella	Tries: Hanno Dirksen, Richard Fussell; Cons: Dan Biggar; Pens: Dan Biggar (2)
11/05/12	Ospreys	45	10	Munster	Liberty Stadium	Tries: Andrew Bishop, Dan Biggar, Hanno Dirksen, Kahn Fotuali'I, Rhys Webb; Cons: Dan Biggar (4); Pens: Dan Biggar (4)
27/05/12	Leinster	30	31	Ospreys	Royal Dublin Society	Tries: Shane Williams (2), Ashley Beck; Cons: Dan Biggar (2); Pens: Dan Biggar (4)

Player	P	W	D	L	Pts	Try	Con	Pen	DG	YC	RC
Morgan Allen	6	3	0	3	0	0	0	0	0	0	0
Scott Baldwin	13	9	0	4	0	0	0	0	0	0	0
Joe Bearman	26	16	2	8	10	2	0	0	0	0	0
Ashley Beck	24	14	2	8	35	7	0	0	0	0	0
Huw Bennett	7	3	1	3	0	0	0	0	0	0	0
Ryan Bevington	20	12	2	6	0	0	0	0	0	1	0
Dan Biggar	28	18	2	8	329	1	45	75	3	3	0
Andrew Bishop	29	20	2	7	10	2	0	0	0	0	0
Tommy Bowe	13	5	2	6	25	5	0	0	0	0	0
Craig Cross	1	0	0	1	0	0	0	0	0	0	0
Barry Davies	11	7	0	4	10	2	0	0	0	0	0
Mefin Davies	14	8	0	6	0	0	0	0	0	0	0
Sam Davies	1	1	0	0	0	0	0	0	0	0	0
Hanno Dirksen	25	18	0	7	40	8	0	0	0	0	0
Ian Evans	21	14	2	5	0	0	0	0	0	2	0
Kahn Fotuali'i	22	12	2	8	15	3	0	0	0	1	0
Richard Fussell	24	17	2	5	15	3	0	0	0	0	0
James Goode	5	4	0	1	0	0	0	0	0	0	0
Ian Gough	17	10	1	6	5	1	0	0	0	2	0
Tom Grabham	3	1	0	2	0	0	0	0	0	0	0
Cai Griffiths	14	8	2	4	0	0	0	0	0	0	0
Tom Habberfield	4	1	0	3	0	0	0	0	0	1	0
Richard Hibbard	26	17	2	7	15	3	0	0	0	2	0
Tom Isaacs	21	17	1	3	10	2	0	0	0	0	0
Paul James	12	8	0	4	5	1	0	0	0	1	0
Aaron Jarvis	23	14	2	7	0	0	0	0	0	0	0
Ben John	2	0	0	2	0	0	0	0	0	0	0
Adam Jones	15	10	0	5	5	1	0	0	0	0	0
Alun Wyn Jones	11	10	1	0	5	1	0	0	0	0	0
Duncan Jones	21	12	2	7	0	0	0	0	0	0	0
Ross Jones	3	1	0	2	5	1	0	0	0	0	0
Ryan Jones	15	8	2	5	10	2	0	0	0	0	0
Richard Kelly	2	0	0	2	0	0	0	0	0	0	0
James King	24	17	0	7	0	0	0	0	0	0	0
Sam Lewis	4	1	0	3	0	0	0	0	0	0	0
Luke Morgan	1	1	0	0	0	0	0	0	0	0	0
Matthew Morgan	22	11	1	10	106	3	11	23	0	0	0
Chauncey O'Toole	5	3	0	2	0	0	0	0	0	1	0
Sonny Parker	13	9	0	4	10	2	0	0	0	0	0
Lloyd Peers	3	1	0	2	0	0	0	0	0	0	0
Kristian Phillips	7	5	0	2	3	0	0	1	0	0	0
Rory Pitman	1	1	0	0	0	0	0	0	0	0	0
Will Price	2	0	0	2	0	0	0	0	0	0	0
Tom Prydie	1	0	0	1	0	0	0	0	0	0	0
Joe Rees	15	10	0	5	0	0	0	0	0	0	0
Tom Smith	29	18	1	10	10	2	0	0	0	5	0
George Stowers	15	6	2	7	5	1	0	0	0	0	0
Will Taylor	1	0	0	1	0	0	0	0	0	0	0
Ben Thomas	1	0	0	1	0	0	0	0	0	0	0
Jonathan Thomas	21	11	2	8	0	0	0	0	0	0	0
Jonny Thomas	1	1	0	0	0	0	0	0	0	0	0
Justin Tipuric	22	15	2	5	10	2	0	0	0	4	0
Eli Walker	5	1	0	4	5	1	0	0	0	0	0
Stefan Watermeyer	1	1	0	0	5	1	0	0	0	0	0
Rhys Webb	28	19	1	8	25	5	0	0	0	0	0
Sam Williams	1	1	0	0	0	0	0	0	0	0	0
Shane Williams	14	8	2	4	17	3	1	0	0	0	0

2012—13 Seasons Results & Player Stats

Date	Team 1			Team 2	Venue	
10/08/12	ASM Clermont Auvergne	49	25	Ospreys	Stade du Mas	
18/08/12	Ospreys	10	21	Bath	Liberty Stadium	
31/08/12	Benetton Rugby Treviso	12	6	Ospreys	Stadio Comunale di Monigo	Pens: Dan Biggar (2)
08/09/12	Ospreys	13	16	Ulster	Liberty Stadium	Tries: Hanno Dirksen; Cons: Matthew Morgan; Pens: Matthew Morgan (2)
14/09/12	Ospreys	10	28	Glasgow Warriors	Liberty Stadium	Tries: Ian Evans; Cons: Dan Biggar; Pens: Dan Biggar
21/09/12	Scarlets	16	23	Ospreys	Parc y Scarlets	Tries: Ryan Jones, Hanno Dirksen; Cons: Dan Biggar (2); Pens: Dan Biggar (3)
29/09/12	Ospreys	30	15	Munster	Liberty Stadium	Tries: Richard Fussell, Richard Hibbard, Penalty Try; Cons: Dan Biggar (3); Pens: Dan Biggar (3)
05/10/12	Zebre Rugby	16	34	Ospreys	Stadio XXV Aprile	Tries: Richard Fussell, Jonathan Thomas, Dan Biggar; Cons: Dan Biggar (2); Pens: Dan Biggar (5)
12/10/12	Ospreys	38	17	Benetton Rugby Treviso	Liberty Stadium	Tries: Hanno Dirksen (2), Ashley Beck, Eli Walker; Cons: Dan Biggar (3); Pens: Dan Biggar (4)
21/10/12	Leicester Tigers	39	22	Ospreys	Welford Road	Tries: Ryan Jones; Cons: Dan Biggar; Pens: Dan Biggar (5)
27/10/12	Ospreys	26	9	Connacht	Liberty Stadium	Tries: Eli Walker, Justin Tipuric, Jonathan Thomas, Kahn Fotuali'I; Cons: Dan Biggar (3)
04/11/12	Ospreys	19	10	Leinster	Liberty Stadium	Tries: Eli Walker; Cons: Matthew Morgan; Pens: Matthew Morgan (3); DG: Matthew Morgan
09/11/12	Ospreys	33	27	Gloucester Rugby	Liberty Stadium	Tries: Tom Grabham, Morgan Allen; Cons: Sam Davies; Pens: Matthew Morgan (4), Sam Davies; DG: Matthew Morgan (2)
17/11/12	Exeter Chiefs	23	13	Ospreys	Sandy Park Stadium	Tries: Morgan Allen; Cons: Sam Davies; Pens: Sam Davies (2)
23/11/12	Edinburgh Rugby	23	13	Ospreys	Murrayfield	Tries: Matthew Morgan; Cons: Matthew Morgan; Pens: Matthew Morgan (2)
30/11/12	Ospreys	33	12	Cardiff Blues	Liberty Stadium	Tries: James King, Richard Fussell, Morgan Allen; Cons: Matthew Morgan (3); Pens: Matthew Morgan (4)
08/12/12	Stade Toulousain	30	14	Ospreys	Stade Ernest-Wallon	Tries: Kahn Fotuali'I, Ryan Bevington; Cons: Dan Biggar, Matthew Morgan
15/12/12	Ospreys	17	6	Stade Toulousain	Liberty Stadium	Tries: Eli Walker; Pens: Dan Biggar (3); DG: Dan Biggar
26/12/12	Ospreys	32	3	Scarlets	Liberty Stadium	Tries: James King, Kahn Fotuali'I, Penalty Try; Cons: Dan Biggar; Pens: Dan Biggar (4); DG: Kahn Fotuali'i
31/12/12	Newport Gwent Dragons	3	14	Ospreys	Rodney Parade	Tries: Eli Walker, Ashley Beck; Cons: Dan Biggar (2)
04/01/13	Ospreys	16	15	Zebre Rugby	Liberty Stadium	Tries: Dan Biggar; Cons: Dan Biggar; Pens: Dan Biggar (3)
13/01/13	Ospreys	15	15	Leicester Tigers	Liberty Stadium	Tries: Joe Bearman, Jonathan Spratt; Cons: Dan Biggar; Pens: Dan Biggar
20/01/13	Benetton Rugby Treviso	17	14	Ospreys	Stadio Comunale di Monigo	Tries: Tom Isaacs; Pens: Dan Biggar (2); DG: Dan Biggar
26/01/13	Newport Gwent Dragons	18	14	Ospreys	Rodney Parade	Tries: Jonathan Thomas; Pens: Matthew Morgan (3)
03/02/13	Ospreys	12	16	Harlequins	Riverside Hardware Brewery Field	Pens: Matthew Morgan (4)
08/02/13	Ulster	12	16	Ospreys	Ravenhill	Tries: Ryan Bevington; Cons: Matthew Morgan; Pens: Matthew Morgan (3)
15/02/13	Connacht	22	10	Ospreys	The Sportsground	Tries: Kahn Fotuali'I; Cons: Matthew Morgan; Pens: Matthew Morgan
22/02/13	Ospreys	24	7	Edinburgh Rugby	Liberty Stadium	Tries: Morgan Allen (2), Rhys Webb; Cons: Matthew Morgan (3); Pens: Matthew Morgan
02/03/13	Munster	13	13	Ospreys	Thomond Park	Tries: Jonathan Thomas; Cons: Matthew Morgan; Pens: Matthew Morgan (2)
22/03/13	Ospreys	52	19	Newport Gwent Dragons	Liberty Stadium	Tries: Kahn Fotuali'I, Tom Habberfield, Ashley Beck, Tom Isaacs, Dan Biggar, Dmitri Arhip, Justin Tipuric; Cons: Dan Biggar (5), Matthew Morgan (2); Pens: Dan Biggar
30/03/13	Cardiff Blues	16	23	Ospreys	Millennium Stadium	Tries: James King, Jonathan Spratt; Cons: Dan Biggar (2); Pens: Dan Biggar (3)
13/04/13	Ospreys	28	3	Benetton Rugby Treviso	Liberty Stadium	Tries: Ben John, Dan Biggar, Rhys Webb; Cons: Dan Biggar (2); Pens: Dan Biggar (3)
19/04/13	Glasgow Warriors	35	17	Ospreys	Scotstoun Stadium	Tries: Cai Griffiths, Sam Lewis; Cons: Dan Biggar (2); Pens: Dan Biggar
03/05/13	Leinster	37	19	Ospreys	Royal Dublin Society	Tries: Dan Biggar, Ben John, Tom Isaacs; Cons: Dan Biggar (2)

Player	P	W	D	L	Pts	Try	Con	Pen	DG	YC	RC
Morgan Allen	14	8	0	6	25	5	0	0	0	2	0
Dmitri Arhip	9	3	1	5	5	1	0	0	0	1	0
Dan Baker	3	1	0	2	0	0	0	0	0	0	0
Scott Baldwin	23	12	2	9	0	0	0	0	0	0	0
Joe Bearman	23	11	1	11	5	1	0	0	0	0	0
Ashley Beck	18	11	1	6	15	3	0	0	0	0	0
Ryan Bevington	24	14	1	9	10	2	0	0	0	1	0
Dan Biggar	21	12	1	8	231	5	34	44	2	0	0
Andrew Bishop	17	10	1	6	0	0	0	0	0	0	0
Sam Davies	3	1	0	2	13	0	2	3	0	0	0
Hanno Dirksen	10	6	0	4	20	4	0	0	0	0	0
Matthew Dwyer	7	3	0	4	0	0	0	0	0	0	0
Nathan Edwards	2	1	0	1	0	0	0	0	0	0	0
Arthur Ellis	4	1	0	3	0	0	0	0	0	0	0
Ian Evans	12	8	0	4	5	1	0	0	0	1	1
Kahn Fotuali'i	25	15	2	8	28	5	0	0	1	0	0
Richard Fussell	28	16	2	10	15	3	0	0	0	0	0
Ian Gough	11	4	1	6	0	0	0	0	0	0	0
Tom Grabham	10	3	0	7	5	1	0	0	0	0	0
Cai Griffiths	8	5	1	2	5	1	0	0	0	0	0
Tom Habberfield	14	7	2	5	5	1	0	0	0	0	0
Dafydd Howells	2	0	0	2	0	0	0	0	0	0	0
Richard Hibbard	17	11	1	5	5	1	0	0	0	0	0
Rhodri Hughes	2	1	0	1	0	0	0	0	0	0	0
Tom Isaacs	24	13	2	9	15	3	0	0	0	0	0
Aaron Jarvis	9	5	0	4	0	0	0	0	0	0	0
Ben John	12	5	0	7	10	2	0	0	0	0	0
Campbell Johnstone	5	1	0	4	0	0	0	0	0	0	0
Adam Jones	15	10	1	4	0	0	0	0	0	3	0
Alun Wyn Jones	17	9	1	7	0	0	0	0	0	1	0
Duncan Jones	28	15	2	11	0	0	0	0	0	1	0
Ross Jones	14	8	0	6	0	0	0	0	0	0	0
Ryan Jones	10	7	1	2	10	2	0	0	0	0	0
James King	24	13	2	9	15	3	0	0	0	2	0
Sam Lewis	18	9	2	7	5	1	0	0	0	2	0
Matthew Morgan	23	11	1	11	131	1	15	29	3	0	0
Jamie Murphy	2	0	0	2	0	0	0	0	0	0	0
Lloyd Peers	20	12	2	6	0	0	0	0	0	0	0
Will Price	2	1	0	1	0	0	0	0	0	0	0
Joe Rees	6	4	0	2	0	0	0	0	0	0	0
Nicky Smith	1	0	0	1	0	0	0	0	0	0	0
Jonathan Spratt	19	9	2	8	10	2	0	0	0	0	0
George Stowers	14	9	0	5	0	0	0	0	0	0	0
Dan Suter	1	0	0	1	0	0	0	0	0	0	0
Jonathan Thomas	21	12	1	8	20	4	0	0	0	1	0
Marc Thomas	7	2	1	4	0	0	0	0	0	0	0
Nicky Thomas	3	1	0	2	0	0	0	0	0	0	0
Justin Tipuric	16	9	1	6	10	2	0	0	0	0	0
Eli Walker	13	9	1	3	25	5	0	0	0	0	0
Rhys Webb	23	11	0	12	10	2	0	0	0	2	0
Owen Williams	2	0	0	2	0	0	0	0	0	1	0
Sam Williams	3	0	0	3	0	0	0	0	0	0	0

All-Time Player List

Name	Played	Debut	Last	Tries	Cons	Pens	DGs	Points	Current	Age On Debut
Morgan Allen	21	29/01/11	03/05/13	6	0	0	0	30	1	20 Years 10 Months 17 Days
Dmitri Arhip	9	30/11/12	03/05/13	1	0	0	0	5	1	24 Years 00 Months 18 Days
Dan Baker	3	26/01/13	22/02/13	0	0	0	0	0	1	20 Years 06 Months 21 Days
Scott Baldwin	39	06/03/09	03/05/13	0	0	0	0	0	1	20 Years 07 Months 22 Days
Lyndon Bateman	79	19/09/03	09/01/09	2	0	0	0	10	0	24 Years 07 Months 17 Days
James Bater	67	05/09/03	26/05/06	6	0	0	0	30	0	23 Years 07 Months 29 Days
Lee Beach	27	12/11/04	12/05/07	1	0	0	0	5	0	22 Years 01 Months 06 Days
Joe Bearman	49	25/09/11	03/05/13	3	0	0	0	15	1	32 Years 06 Months 28 Days
Ashley Beck	71	23/11/07	03/05/13	13	0	0	0	65	1	17 Years 07 Months 08 Days
Huw Bennett	142	29/11/03	22/01/12	8	0	0	0	40	0	20 Years 05 Months 18 Days
Leigh Bevan	2	06/05/08	09/05/08	0	0	0	0	0	0	21 Years 08 Months 02 Days
Ryan Bevington	81	09/05/08	03/05/13	3	0	0	0	15	1	19 Years 05 Months 00 Days
Dan Biggar	125	22/03/08	03/05/13	13	162	265	23	1253	1	18 Years 05 Months 06 Days
Andrew Bishop	188	19/02/05	20/01/13	10	0	0	0	50	1	19 Years 06 Months 12 Days
Dai Bishop	28	03/09/04	03/04/09	4	0	0	0	20	0	20 Years 11 Months 12 Days
Nathan Bonner-Evans	34	05/09/03	18/03/05	2	0	0	0	10	0	24 Years 10 Months 09 Days
Tommy Bowe	77	05/09/08	22/01/12	36	0	0	0	180	0	24 Years 06 Months 14 Days
Matthew Brayley	4	31/01/04	27/02/04	0	0	0	0	0	0	22 Years 04 Months 23 Days
Marc Breeze	4	28/11/08	07/03/10	0	0	0	0	0	0	21 Years 09 Months 17 Days
Aled Brew	24	18/09/04	06/05/08	3	0	0	0	15	0	18 Years 01 Months 09 Days
Lee Byrne	92	02/09/06	23/04/11	27	2	2	0	145	0	26 Years 03 Months 01 Days
Adrian Cashmore	11	14/10/05	17/02/06	4	3	9	0	53	0	32 Years 02 Months 21 Days
Andrew Clatworthy	3	17/10/03	20/02/04	0	0	0	0	0	0	23 Years 00 Months 21 Days
Brent Cockbain	53	03/09/04	30/09/07	1	0	0	0	5	0	29 Years 09 Months 19 Days
Jerry Collins	56	04/09/09	14/05/11	6	0	0	0	30	0	28 Years 10 Months 00 Days
Mike Collins	2	31/08/07	11/09/07	0	0	0	0	0	0	21 Years 01 Months 10 Days
Shaun Connor	100	05/09/03	09/05/08	10	46	97	19	490	0	27 Years 09 Months 16 Days
Craig Cross	5	29/01/11	15/10/11	0	0	0	0	0	0	23 Years 05 Months 17 Days
Alun Wyn Davies	1	31/10/03	31/10/03	0	0	0	0	0	0	19 Years 01 Months 17 Days
Barry Davies	30	04/09/09	22/01/12	3	0	1	0	18	0	28 Years 05 Months 30 Days
Leigh Davies	14	04/09/05	31/03/06	0	0	0	0	0	0	29 Years 06 Months 15 Days
Liam Davies	4	30/10/09	05/12/09	0	0	0	0	0	0	23 Years 05 Months 20 Days
Mefin Davies	33	18/09/04	24/02/12	1	0	0	0	5	0	32 Years 00 Months 16 Days
Ross Davies	2	05/11/09	14/11/09	0	0	0	0	0	0	25 Years 07 Months 11 Days
Sam Davies	4	27/01/12	26/01/13	0	2	3	0	13	1	18 Years 03 Months 21 Days
Des Dillon	7	22/12/05	31/03/06	0	0	0	0	0	0	25 Years 10 Months 27 Days
Hanno Dirksen	42	14/11/09	04/11/12	14	0	0	0	70	1	18 Years 07 Months 14 Days
Ken Dowding	1	02/09/11	02/09/11	0	0	0	0	0	0	26 Years 08 Months 16 Days

Name	Played	Debut	Last	Tries	Cons	Pens	DGs	Points	Current	Age On Debut
Adrian Durston	42	05/09/03	30/04/05	3	0	1	0	18	0	27 Years 10 Months 08 Days
Matthew Dwyer	8	02/09/11	03/02/13	0	0	0	0	0	1	26 Years 07 Months 15 Days
Nathan Edwards	2	09/11/12	26/01/13	0	0	0	0	0	0	20 Years 09 Months 10 Days
Arthur Ellis	4	17/11/12	22/02/13	0	0	0	0	0	0	22 Years 05 Months 10 Days
David Evans	1	15/05/09	15/05/09	0	0	0	0	0	0	20 Years 08 Months 26 Days
Ian Evans	118	10/09/05	19/04/13	2	0	0	0	10	1	20 Years 11 Months 06 Days
Tim Evans	4	06/02/04	05/03/04	0	0	0	0	0	0	22 Years 03 Months 03 Days
Dai Flanagan	5	30/10/10	05/03/11	0	1	6	0	20	0	25 Years 00 Months 06 Days
Kahn Fotuali'i	47	28/10/11	19/04/13	8	0	0	1	43	0	29 Years 05 Months 06 Days
Richard Fussell	81	03/09/10	03/05/13	15	0	0	0	75	1	26 Years 04 Months 22 Days
Rhys Garfield	1	28/11/08	28/11/08	0	0	0	0	0	0	
Scott Gibbs	16	05/09/03	13/02/04	3	0	0	0	15	0	32 Years 07 Months 13 Days
James Goode	15	14/11/09	04/02/12	0	0	0	0	0	0	27 Years 02 Months 09 Days
Ian Gough	119	05/10/07	03/02/13	2	0	0	0	10	1	30 Years 10 Months 25 Days
Tom Grabham	13	15/10/11	22/02/13	1	0	0	0	5	1	20 Years 03 Months 25 Days
Cai Griffiths	123	19/09/03	19/04/13	1	0	0	0	5	0	19 Years 08 Months 14 Days
Tom Habberfield	18	15/10/11	03/05/13	1	0	0	0	5	1	19 Years 04 Months 26 Days
Gavin Henson	98	05/09/03	28/03/09	24	91	160	2	788	0	21 Years 07 Months 04 Days
Richard Hibbard	161	03/09/04	19/04/13	8	0	0	0	40	1	20 Years 08 Months 21 Days
Marty Holah	93	04/11/07	14/05/11	2	0	0	0	10	0	31 Years 01 Months 25 Days
James Hook	107	18/09/04	14/05/11	16	115	155	7	796	0	19 Years 02 Months 22 Days
Pat Horgan	1	12/12/03	12/12/03	0	0	0	0	0	0	30 Years 01 Months 04 Days
Dafydd Howells	2	26/01/13	03/02/13	0	0	0	0	0	1	17 Years 10 Months 04 Days
Rhodri Hughes	2	09/11/12	26/01/13	0	0	0	0	0	1	18 Years 11 Months 14 Days
Tom Isaacs	57	30/10/10	03/05/13	5	0	0	0	25	1	23 Years 08 Months 12 Days
Paul James	180	05/09/03	27/05/12	7	0	0	0	35	0	21 Years 03 Months 23 Days
Ricky Januarie	6	12/12/09	23/01/10	1	0	0	0	5	0	27 Years 10 Months 11 Days
Aaron Jarvis	32	10/09/11	27/10/12	0	0	0	0	0	1	25 Years 03 Months 21 Days
Matthew Jarvis	5	28/11/08	19/11/10	0	2	3	0	13	0	18 Years 03 Months 03 Days
Ben John	16	04/02/10	03/05/13	2	0	0	0	10	1	18 Years 11 Months 07 Days
Campbell Johnstone	5	08/12/12	03/02/13	0	0	0	0	0	0	32 Years 11 Months 01 Days
Adam Jones	176	05/09/03	03/05/13	3	0	0	0	15	1	22 Years 05 Months 28 Days
Alun Wyn Jones	147	04/09/05	03/05/13	11	0	0	0	55	1	19 Years 11 Months 16 Days
Duncan Jones	187	10/01/04	03/05/13	3	0	0	0	15	1	25 Years 03 Months 23 Days
Matt Jones	47	02/01/04	02/03/07	5	19	26	2	147	0	19 Years 08 Months 29 Days
Paul Jones	2	31/10/03	07/11/03	0	0	0	0	0	0	21 Years 04 Months 18 Days
Ross Jones	19	15/10/11	03/05/13	1	0	0	0	5	1	19 Years 09 Months 04 Days
Ryan Jones	136	03/09/04	13/01/13	19	0	0	0	95	1	23 Years 05 Months 21 Days

All-Time Player List (continued)

Name	Played	Debut	Last	Tries	Cons	Pens	DGs	Points	Current	Age On Debut
Damian Karauna	10	09/10/05	29/04/06	1	0	0	0	5	0	30 Years 07 Months 03 Days
Richard Kelly	6	15/05/09	22/10/11	0	0	0	0	0	0	21 Years 08 Months 05 Days
James King	61	30/10/09	03/05/13	3	0	0	0	15	1	19 Years 03 Months 06 Days
Tavis Knoyle	1	30/04/09	30/04/09	0	0	0	0	0	0	18 Years 10 Months 28 Days
Filipo Levi	8	22/02/09	10/05/09	0	0	0	0	0	0	29 Years 05 Months 16 Days
Ben Lewis	24	06/01/07	25/09/10	3	0	0	0	15	0	20 Years 04 Months 11 Days
Sam Lewis	27	15/10/11	03/05/13	1	0	0	0	5	1	21 Years 01 Months 08 Days
Gareth Llewellyn	6	29/11/03	16/01/04	0	0	0	0	0	0	34 Years 09 Months 02 Days
Andy Lloyd	86	31/01/04	19/02/11	3	0	0	0	15	0	22 Years 09 Months 22 Days
Daniel Lloyd-Jones	1	11/09/07	11/09/07	0	0	0	0	0	0	21 Years 02 Months 06 Days
Paul Mackey	1	29/01/05	29/01/05	0	0	0	0	0	0	22 Years 01 Months 08 Days
Justin Marshall	49	02/09/06	02/05/08	10	0	0	1	53	0	33 Years 00 Months 28 Days
Chris Martenko	2	06/01/07	17/02/07	0	0	0	0	0	0	24 Years 00 Months 01 Days
Conor McInerney	5	04/02/10	19/11/10	0	0	0	0	0	0	23 Years 00 Months 16 Days
Andrew Millward	94	05/09/03	26/10/08	4	0	0	0	20	0	30 Years 09 Months 04 Days
Craig Mitchell	35	17/02/06	22/01/11	0	0	0	0	0	0	19 Years 09 Months 14 Days
Luke Morgan	1	27/01/12	27/01/12	0	0	0	0	0	0	19 Years 08 Months 11 Days
Matthew Morgan	50	06/11/10	03/05/13	5	28	62	4	279	1	18 Years 06 Months 14 Days
Gareth Morris	12	12/09/03	16/04/04	3	0	0	0	15	0	26 Years 01 Months 02 Days
Jamie Murphy	2	26/01/13	03/02/13	0	0	0	0	0	1	23 Years 00 Months 28 Days
Richard Mustoe	49	25/09/04	02/03/07	5	0	0	0	25	0	22 Years 09 Months 16 Days
Andrew Newman	75	05/09/03	26/05/06	6	0	0	0	30	0	25 Years 07 Months 29 Days
Jamie Nutbrown	50	09/09/08	05/03/11	4	0	0	0	20	0	27 Years 02 Months 05 Days
Chauncey O'Toole	5	22/10/11	04/02/12	0	0	0	0	0	0	25 Years 08 Months 00 Days
Gareth Owen	50	11/09/07	06/02/11	9	7	9	0	86	0	18 Years 10 Months 06 Days
Sonny Parker	157	03/09/04	10/02/12	29	0	0	0	145	0	27 Years 00 Months 07 Days
Lloyd Peers	24	15/10/11	13/04/13	0	0	0	0	0	1	20 Years 08 Months 13 Days
Kristian Phillips	20	06/05/08	22/10/11	4	0	1	0	23	0	17 Years 08 Months 04 Days
Mike Phillips	60	05/10/07	23/04/11	5	0	0	0	25	0	25 Years 01 Months 06 Days
Rory Pitman	1	27/01/12	27/01/12	0	0	0	0	0	0	22 Years 03 Months 21 Days
Mike Powell	22	15/09/06	09/05/08	0	0	0	0	0	0	27 Years 09 Months 23 Days
Will Price	4	15/10/11	17/11/12	0	0	0	0	0	0	22 Years 11 Months 10 Days
Tom Prydie	12	12/12/09	22/10/11	2	6	0	0	22	0	17 Years 09 Months 19 Days
Richie Pugh	78	05/09/03	11/09/07	7	0	0	0	35	0	20 Years 00 Months 26 Days
Joe Rees	23	12/11/10	09/11/12	0	0	0	0	0	1	20 Years 02 Months 12 Days
Richie Rees	11	12/11/04	17/02/06	2	0	0	0	10	0	21 Years 05 Months 22 Days
Martin Roberts	22	09/10/05	09/05/08	1	0	0	0	5	0	19 Years 04 Months 03 Days
Tal Selley	13	02/09/06	08/05/07	1	0	0	0	5	0	26 Years 04 Months 13 Days

Name	Played	Debut	Last	Tries	Cons	Pens	DGs	Points	Current	Age On Debut
Elvis Seveali'i	42	05/09/03	07/05/05	5	0	0	0	25	0	25 Years 02 Months 16 Days
Ed Shervington	38	22/09/06	14/05/10	1	0	0	0	5	0	21 Years 06 Months 11 Days
Nicky Smith	1	26/01/13	26/01/13	0	0	0	0	0	0	18 Years 09 Months 19 Days
Tom Smith	91	17/02/07	11/05/12	3	0	0	0	15	1	21 Years 02 Months 03 Days
Jason Spice	78	03/09/04	12/05/07	12	1	0	0	62	0	29 Years 08 Months 27 Days
Jonathan Spratt	42	25/11/06	03/05/13	4	0	0	0	20	1	20 Years 06 Months 28 Days
James Storey	21	05/09/03	14/05/04	4	0	0	0	20	0	26 Years 09 Months 10 Days
George Stowers	29	28/10/11	22/03/13	1	0	0	0	5	0	32 Years 08 Months 14 Days
Dan Suter	1	26/01/13	26/01/13	0	0	0	0	0	1	19 Years 06 Months 28 Days
Luke Tait	26	05/09/03	18/03/05	0	0	0	0	0	0	21 Years 10 Months 10 Days
Steve Tandy	102	19/09/03	07/03/10	10	0	0	0	50	0	23 Years 08 Months 03 Days
Mark Taylor	17	31/08/07	09/05/08	0	0	0	0	0	0	34 Years 06 Months 04 Days
Will Taylor	3	29/01/11	02/03/12	0	0	0	0	0	0	19 Years 10 Months 25 Days
Stefan Terblanche	86	07/12/03	05/10/07	16	0	1	1	86	0	28 Years 05 Months 05 Days
Adrian Thomas	2	05/01/08	09/05/08	0	0	0	0	0	0	26 Years 06 Months 21 Days
Ben Thomas	1	15/10/11	15/10/11	0	0	0	0	0	0	20 Years 08 Months 20 Days
Gavin Thomas	15	05/09/03	16/01/04	1	0	0	0	5	0	25 Years 10 Months 14 Days
Jonathan Thomas	188	29/11/03	19/04/13	14	0	0	0	70	0	20 Years 11 Months 02 Days
Jonny Thomas	1	27/01/12	27/01/12	0	0	0	0	0	0	27 Years 10 Months 18 Days
Marc Thomas	7	04/11/12	19/04/13	0	0	0	0	0	1	22 Years 03 Months 20 Days
Nicky Thomas	3	30/10/09	14/11/09	0	0	0	0	0	0	25 Years 05 Months 18 Days
Nicky Thomas	3	09/11/12	23/11/12	0	0	0	0	0	0	18 Years 02 Months 14 Days
Filo Tiatia	99	02/09/06	29/05/10	10	0	0	0	50	0	35 Years 02 Months 29 Days
Justin Tipuric	67	05/11/09	03/05/13	7	0	0	0	35	1	20 Years 02 Months 30 Days
Dave Tiueti	38	05/09/03	06/03/05	8	0	0	0	40	0	30 Years 02 Months 30 Days
Hale T-Pole	8	27/10/07	09/05/08	0	0	0	0	0	0	28 Years 05 Months 27 Days
Jonny Vaughton	63	10/09/05	07/03/10	11	0	0	0	55	0	23 Years 07 Months 20 Days
Eli Walker	28	25/09/10	13/01/13	7	0	0	0	35	1	18 Years 05 Months 28 Days
Nikki Walker	103	02/09/06	14/05/11	37	0	0	0	185	0	24 Years 05 Months 28 Days
Stefan Watermeyer	2	27/01/12	24/02/12	1	0	0	0	5	0	23 Years 07 Months 24 Days
Rhys Webb	91	28/03/08	03/05/13	8	0	0	0	40	1	19 Years 03 Months 19 Days
Chris Wells	11	05/09/03	18/12/04	1	0	0	0	5	0	26 Years 06 Months 24 Days
Rhodri Wells	23	17/10/03	30/10/09	1	0	0	0	5	0	19 Years 06 Months 26 Days
Andy Williams	34	05/09/03	05/11/04	3	0	0	0	15	0	22 Years 06 Months 29 Days
Barry Williams	101	05/09/03	14/10/07	8	0	0	0	40	0	29 Years 07 Months 30 Days
Owen Williams	2	17/11/12	23/11/12	0	0	0	0	0	0	30 Years 09 Months 14 Days
Sam Williams	4	27/01/12	03/02/13	0	0	0	0	0	1	22 Years 02 Months 17 Days
Shane Williams	141	29/11/03	27/05/12	57	1	0	2	293	0	26 Years 09 Months 03 Days

Top 10 Appearances

Name	Played	Debut	Last	Tries	Cons	Pens	DGs	Points	Current	Age On Debut
Andrew Bishop	188	19/02/05	20/01/13	10	0	0	0	50	1	19 Years 06 Months 12 Days
Jonathan Thomas	188	29/11/03	19/04/13	14	0	0	0	70	0	20 Years 11 Months 02 Days
Duncan Jones	187	10/01/04	03/05/13	3	0	0	0	15	1	25 Years 03 Months 23 Days
Paul James	180	05/09/03	27/05/12	7	0	0	0	35	0	21 Years 03 Months 23 Days
Adam Jones	176	05/09/03	03/05/13	3	0	0	0	15	1	22 Years 05 Months 28 Days
Richard Hibbard	161	03/09/04	19/04/13	8	0	0	0	40	1	20 Years 08 Months 21 Days
Sonny Parker	157	03/09/04	10/02/12	29	0	0	0	145	0	27 Years 00 Months 07 Days
Alun Wyn Jones	147	04/09/05	03/05/13	11	0	0	0	55	1	19 Years 11 Months 16 Days
Huw Bennett	142	29/11/03	22/01/12	8	0	0	0	40	0	20 Years 05 Months 18 Days
Shane Williams	141	29/11/03	27/05/12	57	1	0	2	293	0	26 Years 09 Months 03 Days

Top 10 Points Scorers

Name	Played	Debut	Last	Tries	Cons	Pens	DGs	Points	Current	Age On Debut
Dan Biggar	125	22/03/08	03/05/13	13	162	265	23	1253	1	18 Years 05 Months 06 Days
James Hook	107	18/09/04	14/05/11	16	115	155	7	796	0	19 Years 02 Months 22 Days
Gavin Henson	98	05/09/03	28/03/09	24	91	160	2	788	0	21 Years 07 Months 04 Days
Shaun Connor	100	05/09/03	09/05/08	10	46	97	19	490	0	27 Years 09 Months 16 Days
Shane Williams	141	29/11/03	27/05/12	57	1	0	2	293	0	26 Years 09 Months 03 Days
Matthew Morgan	50	06/11/10	03/05/13	5	28	62	4	279	1	18 Years 06 Months 14 Days
Nikki Walker	103	02/09/06	14/05/11	37	0	0	0	185	0	24 Years 05 Months 28 Days
Tommy Bowe	77	05/09/08	22/01/12	36	0	0	0	180	0	24 Years 06 Months 14 Days
Matt Jones	47	02/01/04	02/03/07	5	19	26	2	147	0	19 Years 08 Months 29 Days
Lee Byrne	92	02/09/06	23/04/11	27	2	2	0	145	0	26 Years 03 Months 01 Days
Sonny Parker	157	03/09/04	10/02/12	29	0	0	0	145	0	27 Years 00 Months 07 Days

Top 10 Try Scorers

Name	Played	Debut	Last	Tries	Cons	Pens	DGs	Points	Current	Age On Debut
Shane Williams	141	29/11/03	27/05/12	57	1	0	2	293	0	26 Years 09 Months 03 Days
Nikki Walker	103	02/09/06	14/05/11	37	0	0	0	185	0	24 Years 05 Months 28 Days
Tommy Bowe	77	05/09/08	22/01/12	36	0	0	0	180	0	24 Years 06 Months 14 Days
Sonny Parker	157	03/09/04	10/02/12	29	0	0	0	145	0	27 Years 00 Months 07 Days
Lee Byrne	92	02/09/06	23/04/11	27	2	2	0	145	0	26 Years 03 Months 01 Days
Gavin Henson	98	05/09/03	28/03/09	24	91	160	2	788	0	21 Years 07 Months 04 Days
Ryan Jones	136	03/09/04	13/01/13	19	0	0	0	95	1	23 Years 05 Months 21 Days
James Hook	107	18/09/04	14/05/11	16	115	155	7	796	0	19 Years 02 Months 22 Days
Stefan Terblanche	86	07/12/03	05/10/07	16	0	1	1	86	0	28 Years 05 Months 05 Days
Richard Fussell	81	03/09/10	03/05/13	15	0	0	0	75	1	26 Years 04 Months 22 Days

International Players

Name	DOB	Country
Dmitri Arhip	12/11/1988	Moldova
Dan Baker	05/07/1992	Wales
Scott Baldwin	12/07/1988	Wales
James Bater	07/01/1980	Wales
Ashley Beck	15/04/1990	Wales
Huw Bennett	11/06/1983	Wales
Ryan Bevington	09/12/1988	Wales
Dan Biggar	16/10/1989	Wales
Andrew Bishop	07/08/1985	Wales
Tommy Bowe	22/02/1984	Ireland
Aled Brew	09/08/1986	Wales
Lee Byrne	01/06/1980	Wales
Brent Cockbain	15/11/1974	Wales
Mefin Davies	02/09/1972	Wales
Ian Evans	04/10/1984	Wales
Kahn Fotuali'i	22/05/1982	Samoa
Ian Gough	10/11/1976	Wales
Gavin Henson	01/02/1982	Wales
Richard Hibbard	13/12/1983	Wales
James Hook	27/06/1985	Wales
Dafydd Howells	22/03/1995	Wales
Paul James	13/05/1982	Wales
Aaron Jarvis	20/05/1986	Wales
Adam Jones	08/03/1981	Wales
Alun Wyn Jones	19/09/1985	Wales
Duncan Jones	18/09/1978	Wales
Matt Jones	04/04/1984	Wales
Ryan Jones	13/03/1981	Wales
James King	24/07/1990	Wales
Filipo Levi	06/09/1979	Samoa
Gareth Llewellyn	27/02/1969	Wales
Craig Mitchell	03/05/1986	Wales
Chauncey O'Toole	22/02/1986	Canada
Sonny Parker	27/08/1977	Wales

Name	DOB	Country
Mike Phillips	29/08/1982	Wales
Tom Prydie	23/02/1992	Wales
Richie Pugh	10/08/1983	Wales
Elvis Seveali'i	20/06/1978	Samoa
Jonathan Spratt	28/04/1986	Wales
Gavin Thomas	22/10/1977	Wales
Jonathan Thomas	27/12/1982	Wales
Justin Tipuric	06/08/1989	Wales
Hale T-Pole	30/04/1979	Tonga
Nikki Walker	05/03/1982	Scotland
Rhys Webb	09/12/1988	Wales
Andy Williams	07/02/1981	Wales
Shane Williams	26/02/1977	Wales

British & Irish Lions

Name	Year
Brent Cockbain	2005
Gavin Henson	2005
Ryan Jones	2005, 2009
Shane Williams	2005, 2009
Tommy Bowe	2009
Lee Byrne	2009
James Hook	2009
Adam Jones	2009, 2013
Alun Wyn Jones	2009, 2013
Mike Phillips	2009
Ian Evans	2013
Richard Hibbard	2013
Justin Tipuric	2013

All statistics correct up to 1/8/13

Acknowledgements

I would just like to say a very big thank you to the following people, without whose help it wouldn't have been possible to have got the official history of the first ten years of Ospreys Rugby into print:

Andrew Hore, Roger Blyth and Dani Delamere at the Ospreys for their constant encouragement and support; Lefi Gruffudd, Eirian Jones and Alan Thomas at Y Lolfa, whose expertise and understanding in guiding me through the entire process made this book possible; everybody at Sportstat, official statisticians of Ospreys Rugby, without whom this book would be missing some vital information. In particular, I'd like to thank Rhys Bradfield for his efforts and assistance.

I also owe a debt of gratitude to Natasha Fulford and her colleagues at MGB PR in Swansea, architects of the Ospreys brand and the brains behind the mask at the inception of the region, for opening up their archives from the formative days of Ospreys Rugby.

I would also like to say a special thanks to my partner, Gaynor, for her ongoing support, patience and understanding while I was putting the book together, and to my son, Laurie, for providing the motivation and inspiration. Thank you both.

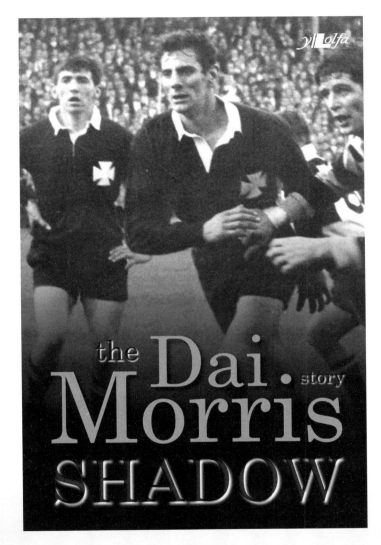

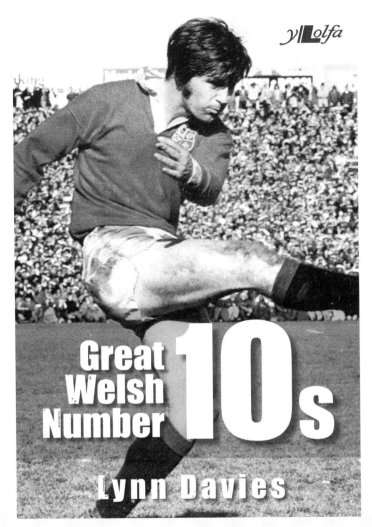

Ten Years of the Ospreys is just one of a whole range of publications from Y Lolfa. For a full list of books currently in print, send now for your free copy of our new full-colour catalogue. Or simply surf into our website

www.ylolfa.com

for secure on-line ordering.

TALYBONT CEREDIGION CYMRU SY24 5HE
e-mail ylolfa@ylolfa.com
website www.ylolfa.com
phone (01970) 832 304
fax 832 782